T0325403

THIS IS YOUR **PASSBOOK®** FOR ...

STATIONARY ENGINEER (ELECTRIC)

NLC®

NATIONAL LEARNING CORPORATION®

passbooks.com

PASSBOOK® SERIES

THE *PASSBOOK® SERIES* has been created to prepare applicants and candidates for the ultimate academic battlefield – the examination room.

At some time in our lives, each and every one of us may be required to take an examination – for validation, matriculation, admission, qualification, registration, certification, or licensure.

Based on the assumption that every applicant or candidate has met the basic formal educational standards, has taken the required number of courses, and read the necessary texts, the *PASSBOOK® SERIES* furnishes the one special preparation which may assure passing with confidence, instead of failing with insecurity. Examination questions – together with answers – are furnished as the basic vehicle for study so that the mysteries of the examination and its compounding difficulties may be eliminated or diminished by a sure method.

This book is meant to help you pass your examination provided that you qualify and are serious in your objective.

The entire field is reviewed through the huge store of content information which is succinctly presented through a provocative and challenging approach – the question-and-answer method.

A climate of success is established by furnishing the correct answers at the end of each test.

You soon learn to recognize types of questions, forms of questions, and patterns of questioning. You may even begin to anticipate expected outcomes.

You perceive that many questions are repeated or adapted so that you can gain acute insights, which may enable you to score many sure points.

You learn how to confront new questions, or types of questions, and to attack them confidently and work out the correct answers.

You note objectives and emphases, and recognize pitfalls and dangers, so that you may make positive educational adjustments.

Moreover, you are kept fully informed in relation to new concepts, methods, practices, and directions in the field.

You discover that you arre actually taking the examination all the time: you are preparing for the examination by "taking" an examination, not by reading extraneous and/or supererogatory textbooks.

In short, this PASSBOOK®, used directedly, should be an important factor in helping you to pass your test.

STATIONARY ENGINEER (ELECTRIC)

DUTIES

Stationary Engineers (Electric), under general supervision, operate, inspect, and adjust high and/or low voltage electrically powered plant equipment including diesel engines. They operate, inspect, maintain, repair, test and adjust equipment such as: generators, pumps, transformers, electric motors, bearings, switchboards, controllers, compressors, meters, gauges, valves, fittings, heating apparatus, converters, rectifiers, controls, circuit breakers, etc.; operate dual and tri-fuel engines, generators, pumps, blowers, high tension switchboards and electrical equipment (permanent and portable); they oil, clean, and make minor repairs to this equipment; read meters, gauges, and recording devices; keep records; prepare reports; take responsible charge of a watch, and while so engaged are responsible for and direct subordinate personnel; instruct and guide subordinates and other personnel; oversee the corrective and preventive maintenance of equipment and structures; perform inspections and assessments of assigned facility; may monitor telemetry of collection system operations; direct operations to prevent bypassing; maintain combined sewer overflow retention facilities, inflatable damn in-line storage facilities, and in-situ aeration of water bodies; may operate a motor vehicle; and perform related work.

SCOPE OF THE EXAMINATION

The multiple-choice test may include questions on job related mathematics; fundamentals of electronics, electric circuits and machines; instrumentation and control fundamentals, and computer operations and logic; operation, maintenance, troubleshooting and repair of electric motors, generators, internal combustion engines, diesel engines, pumps, compressors, blowers, boilers and HVAC equipment and systems, and hydraulic and auxiliary equipment;   principles of supervision; record keeping and report writing; safety; standards of proper employee ethical conduct, and other related areas.

HOW TO TAKE A TEST

I. YOU MUST PASS AN EXAMINATION

A. *WHAT EVERY CANDIDATE SHOULD KNOW*

Examination applicants often ask us for help in preparing for the written test. What can I study in advance? What kinds of questions will be asked? How will the test be given? How will the papers be graded?

As an applicant for a civil service examination, you may be wondering about some of these things. Our purpose here is to suggest effective methods of advance study and to describe civil service examinations.

Your chances for success on this examination can be increased if you know how to prepare. Those "pre-examination jitters" can be reduced if you know what to expect. You can even experience an adventure in good citizenship if you know why civil service exams are given.

B. *WHY ARE CIVIL SERVICE EXAMINATIONS GIVEN?*

Civil service examinations are important to you in two ways. As a citizen, you want public jobs filled by employees who know how to do their work. As a job seeker, you want a fair chance to compete for that job on an equal footing with other candidates. The best-known means of accomplishing this two-fold goal is the competitive examination.

Exams are widely publicized throughout the nation. They may be administered for jobs in federal, state, city, municipal, town or village governments or agencies.

Any citizen may apply, with some limitations, such as the age or residence of applicants. Your experience and education may be reviewed to see whether you meet the requirements for the particular examination. When these requirements exist, they are reasonable and applied consistently to all applicants. Thus, a competitive examination may cause you some uneasiness now, but it is your privilege and safeguard.

C. *HOW ARE CIVIL SERVICE EXAMS DEVELOPED?*

Examinations are carefully written by trained technicians who are specialists in the field known as "psychological measurement," in consultation with recognized authorities in the field of work that the test will cover. These experts recommend the subject matter areas or skills to be tested; only those knowledges or skills important to your success on the job are included. The most reliable books and source materials available are used as references. Together, the experts and technicians judge the difficulty level of the questions.

Test technicians know how to phrase questions so that the problem is clearly stated. Their ethics do not permit "trick" or "catch" questions. Questions may have been tried out on sample groups, or subjected to statistical analysis, to determine their usefulness.

Written tests are often used in combination with performance tests, ratings of training and experience, and oral interviews. All of these measures combine to form the best-known means of finding the right person for the right job.

II. HOW TO PASS THE WRITTEN TEST

A. *NATURE OF THE EXAMINATION*

To prepare intelligently for civil service examinations, you should know how they differ from school examinations you have taken. In school you were assigned certain definite pages to read or subjects to cover. The examination questions were quite detailed and usually emphasized memory. Civil service exams, on the other hand, try to discover your present ability to perform the duties of a position, plus your potentiality to learn these duties. In other words, a civil service exam attempts to predict how successful you will be. Questions cover such a broad area that they cannot be as minute and detailed as school exam questions.

In the public service similar kinds of work, or positions, are grouped together in one "class." This process is known as *position-classification*. All the positions in a class are paid according to the salary range for that class. One class title covers all of these positions, and they are all tested by the same examination.

B. *FOUR BASIC STEPS*

1) Study the announcement

How, then, can you know what subjects to study? Our best answer is: "Learn as much as possible about the class of positions for which you've applied." The exam will test the knowledge, skills and abilities needed to do the work.

Your most valuable source of information about the position you want is the official exam announcement. This announcement lists the training and experience qualifications. Check these standards and apply only if you come reasonably close to meeting them.

The brief description of the position in the examination announcement offers some clues to the subjects which will be tested. Think about the job itself. Review the duties in your mind. Can you perform them, or are there some in which you are rusty? Fill in the blank spots in your preparation.

Many jurisdictions preview the written test in the exam announcement by including a section called "Knowledge and Abilities Required," "Scope of the Examination," or some similar heading. Here you will find out specifically what fields will be tested.

2) Review your own background

Once you learn in general what the position is all about, and what you need to know to do the work, ask yourself which subjects you already know fairly well and which need improvement. You may wonder whether to concentrate on improving your strong areas or on building some background in your fields of weakness. When the announcement has specified "some knowledge" or "considerable knowledge," or has used adjectives like "beginning principles of…" or "advanced … methods," you can get a clue as to the number and difficulty of questions to be asked in any given field. More questions, and hence broader coverage, would be included for those subjects which are more important in the work. Now weigh your strengths and weaknesses against the job requirements and prepare accordingly.

3) Determine the level of the position

Another way to tell how intensively you should prepare is to understand the level of the job for which you are applying. Is it the entering level? In other words, is this the position in which beginners in a field of work are hired? Or is it an intermediate or advanced level? Sometimes this is indicated by such words as "Junior" or "Senior" in the class title. Other jurisdictions use Roman numerals to designate the level – Clerk I, Clerk II, for example. The word "Supervisor" sometimes appears in the title. If the level is not indicated by the title, check the description of duties. Will you be working under very close supervision, or will you have responsibility for independent decisions in this work?

4) Choose appropriate study materials

Now that you know the subjects to be examined and the relative amount of each subject to be covered, you can choose suitable study materials. For beginning level jobs, or even advanced ones, if you have a pronounced weakness in some aspect of your training, read a modern, standard textbook in that field. Be sure it is up to date and has general coverage. Such books are normally available at your library, and the librarian will be glad to help you locate one. For entry-level positions, questions of appropriate difficulty are chosen – neither highly advanced questions, nor those too simple. Such questions require careful thought but not advanced training.

If the position for which you are applying is technical or advanced, you will read more advanced, specialized material. If you are already familiar with the basic principles of your field, elementary textbooks would waste your time. Concentrate on advanced textbooks and technical periodicals. Think through the concepts and review difficult problems in your field.

These are all general sources. You can get more ideas on your own initiative, following these leads. For example, training manuals and publications of the government agency which employs workers in your field can be useful, particularly for technical and professional positions. A letter or visit to the government department involved may result in more specific study suggestions, and certainly will provide you with a more definite idea of the exact nature of the position you are seeking.

III. KINDS OF TESTS

Tests are used for purposes other than measuring knowledge and ability to perform specified duties. For some positions, it is equally important to test ability to make adjustments to new situations or to profit from training. In others, basic mental abilities not dependent on information are essential. Questions which test these things may not appear as pertinent to the duties of the position as those which test for knowledge and information. Yet they are often highly important parts of a fair examination. For very general questions, it is almost impossible to help you direct your study efforts. What we can do is to point out some of the more common of these general abilities needed in public service positions and describe some typical questions.

1) General information

Broad, general information has been found useful for predicting job success in some kinds of work. This is tested in a variety of ways, from vocabulary lists to questions about current events. Basic background in some field of work, such as sociology or economics, may be sampled in a group of questions. Often these are principles which have become familiar to most persons through exposure rather than through formal training. It is difficult to advise you how to study for these questions; being alert to the world around you is our best suggestion.

2) Verbal ability

An example of an ability needed in many positions is verbal or language ability. Verbal ability is, in brief, the ability to use and understand words. Vocabulary and grammar tests are typical measures of this ability. Reading comprehension or paragraph interpretation questions are common in many kinds of civil service tests. You are given a paragraph of written material and asked to find its central meaning.

3) Numerical ability

Number skills can be tested by the familiar arithmetic problem, by checking paired lists of numbers to see which are alike and which are different, or by interpreting charts and graphs. In the latter test, a graph may be printed in the test booklet which you are asked to use as the basis for answering questions.

4) Observation

A popular test for law-enforcement positions is the observation test. A picture is shown to you for several minutes, then taken away. Questions about the picture test your ability to observe both details and larger elements.

5) Following directions

In many positions in the public service, the employee must be able to carry out written instructions dependably and accurately. You may be given a chart with several columns, each column listing a variety of information. The questions require you to carry out directions involving the information given in the chart.

6) Skills and aptitudes

Performance tests effectively measure some manual skills and aptitudes. When the skill is one in which you are trained, such as typing or shorthand, you can practice. These tests are often very much like those given in business school or high school courses. For many of the other skills and aptitudes, however, no short-time preparation can be made. Skills and abilities natural to you or that you have developed throughout your lifetime are being tested.

Many of the general questions just described provide all the data needed to answer the questions and ask you to use your reasoning ability to find the answers. Your best preparation for these tests, as well as for tests of facts and ideas, is to be at your physical and mental best. You, no doubt, have your own methods of getting into an exam-taking mood and keeping "in shape." The next section lists some ideas on this subject.

IV. KINDS OF QUESTIONS

Only rarely is the "essay" question, which you answer in narrative form, used in civil service tests. Civil service tests are usually of the short-answer type. Full instructions for answering these questions will be given to you at the examination. But in case this is your first experience with short-answer questions and separate answer sheets, here is what you need to know:

1) Multiple-choice Questions

Most popular of the short-answer questions is the "multiple choice" or "best answer" question. It can be used, for example, to test for factual knowledge, ability to solve problems or judgment in meeting situations found at work.

A multiple-choice question is normally one of three types—

- It can begin with an incomplete statement followed by several possible endings. You are to find the one ending which *best* completes the statement, although some of the others may not be entirely wrong.
- It can also be a complete statement in the form of a question which is answered by choosing one of the statements listed.
- It can be in the form of a problem – again you select the best answer.

Here is an example of a multiple-choice question with a discussion which should give you some clues as to the method for choosing the right answer:

When an employee has a complaint about his assignment, the action which will *best* help him overcome his difficulty is to
- A. discuss his difficulty with his coworkers
- B. take the problem to the head of the organization
- C. take the problem to the person who gave him the assignment
- D. say nothing to anyone about his complaint

In answering this question, you should study each of the choices to find which is best. Consider choice "A" – Certainly an employee may discuss his complaint with fellow employees, but no change or improvement can result, and the complaint remains unresolved. Choice "B" is a poor choice since the head of the organization probably does not know what assignment you have been given, and taking your problem to him is known as "going over the head" of the supervisor. The supervisor, or person who made the assignment, is the person who can clarify it or correct any injustice. Choice "C" is, therefore, correct. To say nothing, as in choice "D," is unwise. Supervisors have and interest in knowing the problems employees are facing, and the employee is seeking a solution to his problem.

2) True/False Questions

The "true/false" or "right/wrong" form of question is sometimes used. Here a complete statement is given. Your job is to decide whether the statement is right or wrong.

SAMPLE: A roaming cell-phone call to a nearby city costs less than a non-roaming call to a distant city.

This statement is wrong, or false, since roaming calls are more expensive.
This is not a complete list of all possible question forms, although most of the others are variations of these common types. You will always get complete directions for

answering questions. Be sure you understand *how* to mark your answers – ask questions until you do.

V. RECORDING YOUR ANSWERS

Computer terminals are used more and more today for many different kinds of exams.

For an examination with very few applicants, you may be told to record your answers in the test booklet itself. Separate answer sheets are much more common. If this separate answer sheet is to be scored by machine – and this is often the case – it is highly important that you mark your answers correctly in order to get credit.

An electronic scoring machine is often used in civil service offices because of the speed with which papers can be scored. Machine-scored answer sheets must be marked with a pencil, which will be given to you. This pencil has a high graphite content which responds to the electronic scoring machine. As a matter of fact, stray dots may register as answers, so do not let your pencil rest on the answer sheet while you are pondering the correct answer. Also, if your pencil lead breaks or is otherwise defective, ask for another.

Since the answer sheet will be dropped in a slot in the scoring machine, be careful not to bend the corners or get the paper crumpled.

The answer sheet normally has five vertical columns of numbers, with 30 numbers to a column. These numbers correspond to the question numbers in your test booklet. After each number, going across the page are four or five pairs of dotted lines. These short dotted lines have small letters or numbers above them. The first two pairs may also have a "T" or "F" above the letters. This indicates that the first two pairs only are to be used if the questions are of the true-false type. If the questions are multiple choice, disregard the "T" and "F" and pay attention only to the small letters or numbers.

Answer your questions in the manner of the sample that follows:

32. The largest city in the United States is
    A. Washington, D.C.
    B. New York City
    C. Chicago
    D. Detroit
    E. San Francisco

1) Choose the answer you think is best. (New York City is the largest, so "B" is correct.)
2) Find the row of dotted lines numbered the same as the question you are answering. (Find row number 32)
3) Find the pair of dotted lines corresponding to the answer. (Find the pair of lines under the mark "B.")
4) Make a solid black mark between the dotted lines.

VI. BEFORE THE TEST

Common sense will help you find procedures to follow to get ready for an examination. Too many of us, however, overlook these sensible measures. Indeed, nervousness and fatigue have been found to be the most serious reasons why applicants fail to do their best on civil service tests. Here is a list of reminders:

- Begin your preparation early – Don't wait until the last minute to go scurrying around for books and materials or to find out what the position is all about.
- Prepare continuously – An hour a night for a week is better than an all-night cram session. This has been definitely established. What is more, a night a week for a month will return better dividends than crowding your study into a shorter period of time.
- Locate the place of the exam – You have been sent a notice telling you when and where to report for the examination. If the location is in a different town or otherwise unfamiliar to you, it would be well to inquire the best route and learn something about the building.
- Relax the night before the test – Allow your mind to rest. Do not study at all that night. Plan some mild recreation or diversion; then go to bed early and get a good night's sleep.
- Get up early enough to make a leisurely trip to the place for the test – This way unforeseen events, traffic snarls, unfamiliar buildings, etc. will not upset you.
- Dress comfortably – A written test is not a fashion show. You will be known by number and not by name, so wear something comfortable.
- Leave excess paraphernalia at home – Shopping bags and odd bundles will get in your way. You need bring only the items mentioned in the official notice you received; usually everything you need is provided. Do not bring reference books to the exam. They will only confuse those last minutes and be taken away from you when in the test room.
- Arrive somewhat ahead of time – If because of transportation schedules you must get there very early, bring a newspaper or magazine to take your mind off yourself while waiting.
- Locate the examination room – When you have found the proper room, you will be directed to the seat or part of the room where you will sit. Sometimes you are given a sheet of instructions to read while you are waiting. Do not fill out any forms until you are told to do so; just read them and be prepared.
- Relax and prepare to listen to the instructions
- If you have any physical problem that may keep you from doing your best, be sure to tell the test administrator. If you are sick or in poor health, you really cannot do your best on the exam. You can come back and take the test some other time.

VII. AT THE TEST

The day of the test is here and you have the test booklet in your hand. The temptation to get going is very strong. Caution! There is more to success than knowing the right answers. You must know how to identify your papers and understand variations in the type of short-answer question used in this particular examination. Follow these suggestions for maximum results from your efforts:

1) Cooperate with the monitor

The test administrator has a duty to create a situation in which you can be as much at ease as possible. He will give instructions, tell you when to begin, check to see that you are marking your answer sheet correctly, and so on. He is not there to guard you, although he will see that your competitors do not take unfair advantage. He wants to help you do your best.

2) Listen to all instructions

Don't jump the gun! Wait until you understand all directions. In most civil service tests you get more time than you need to answer the questions. So don't be in a hurry. Read each word of instructions until you clearly understand the meaning. Study the examples, listen to all announcements and follow directions. Ask questions if you do not understand what to do.

3) Identify your papers

Civil service exams are usually identified by number only. You will be assigned a number; you must not put your name on your test papers. Be sure to copy your number correctly. Since more than one exam may be given, copy your exact examination title.

4) Plan your time

Unless you are told that a test is a "speed" or "rate of work" test, speed itself is usually not important. Time enough to answer all the questions will be provided, but this does not mean that you have all day. An overall time limit has been set. Divide the total time (in minutes) by the number of questions to determine the approximate time you have for each question.

5) Do not linger over difficult questions

If you come across a difficult question, mark it with a paper clip (useful to have along) and come back to it when you have been through the booklet. One caution if you do this – be sure to skip a number on your answer sheet as well. Check often to be sure that you have not lost your place and that you are marking in the row numbered the same as the question you are answering.

6) Read the questions

Be sure you know what the question asks! Many capable people are unsuccessful because they failed to *read* the questions correctly.

7) Answer all questions

Unless you have been instructed that a penalty will be deducted for incorrect answers, it is better to guess than to omit a question.

8) Speed tests

It is often better NOT to guess on speed tests. It has been found that on timed tests people are tempted to spend the last few seconds before time is called in marking answers at random – without even reading them – in the hope of picking up a few extra points. To discourage this practice, the instructions may warn you that your score will be "corrected" for guessing. That is, a penalty will be applied. The incorrect answers will be deducted from the correct ones, or some other penalty formula will be used.

9) Review your answers

If you finish before time is called, go back to the questions you guessed or omitted to give them further thought. Review other answers if you have time.

10) Return your test materials

If you are ready to leave before others have finished or time is called, take ALL your materials to the monitor and leave quietly. Never take any test material with you. The monitor can discover whose papers are not complete, and taking a test booklet may be grounds for disqualification.

VIII. EXAMINATION TECHNIQUES

1) Read the general instructions carefully. These are usually printed on the first page of the exam booklet. As a rule, these instructions refer to the timing of the examination; the fact that you should not start work until the signal and must stop work at a signal, etc. If there are any *special* instructions, such as a choice of questions to be answered, make sure that you note this instruction carefully.

2) When you are ready to start work on the examination, that is as soon as the signal has been given, read the instructions to each question booklet, underline any key words or phrases, such as *least, best, outline, describe* and the like. In this way you will tend to answer as requested rather than discover on reviewing your paper that you *listed without describing*, that you selected the *worst* choice rather than the *best* choice, etc.

3) If the examination is of the objective or multiple-choice type – that is, each question will also give a series of possible answers: A, B, C or D, and you are called upon to select the best answer and write the letter next to that answer on your answer paper – it is advisable to start answering each question in turn. There may be anywhere from 50 to 100 such questions in the three or four hours allotted and you can see how much time would be taken if you read through all the questions before beginning to answer any. Furthermore, if you come across a question or group of questions which you know would be difficult to answer, it would undoubtedly affect your handling of all the other questions.

4) If the examination is of the essay type and contains but a few questions, it is a moot point as to whether you should read all the questions before starting to answer any one. Of course, if you are given a choice – say five out of seven and the like – then it is essential to read all the questions so you can eliminate the two that are most difficult. If, however, you are asked to answer all the questions, there may be danger in trying to answer the easiest one first because you may find that you will spend too much time on it. The best technique is to answer the first question, then proceed to the second, etc.

5) Time your answers. Before the exam begins, write down the time it started, then add the time allowed for the examination and write down the time it must be completed, then divide the time available somewhat as follows:

- If 3-1/2 hours are allowed, that would be 210 minutes. If you have 80 objective-type questions, that would be an average of 2-1/2 minutes per question. Allow yourself no more than 2 minutes per question, or a total of 160 minutes, which will permit about 50 minutes to review.
- If for the time allotment of 210 minutes there are 7 essay questions to answer, that would average about 30 minutes a question. Give yourself only 25 minutes per question so that you have about 35 minutes to review.

6) The most important instruction is to *read each question* and make sure you know what is wanted. The second most important instruction is to *time yourself properly* so that you answer every question. The third most important instruction is to *answer every question*. Guess if you have to but include something for each question. Remember that you will receive no credit for a blank and will probably receive some credit if you write something in answer to an essay question. If you guess a letter – say "B" for a multiple-choice question – you may have guessed right. If you leave a blank as an answer to a multiple-choice question, the examiners may respect your feelings but it will not add a point to your score. Some exams may penalize you for wrong answers, so in such cases *only*, you may not want to guess unless you have some basis for your answer.

7) Suggestions
   a. Objective-type questions
      1. Examine the question booklet for proper sequence of pages and questions
      2. Read all instructions carefully
      3. Skip any question which seems too difficult; return to it after all other questions have been answered
      4. Apportion your time properly; do not spend too much time on any single question or group of questions
      5. Note and underline key words – *all, most, fewest, least, best, worst, same, opposite,* etc.
      6. Pay particular attention to negatives
      7. Note unusual option, e.g., unduly long, short, complex, different or similar in content to the body of the question
      8. Observe the use of "hedging" words – *probably, may, most likely,* etc.
      9. Make sure that your answer is put next to the same number as the question
      10. Do not second-guess unless you have good reason to believe the second answer is definitely more correct
      11. Cross out original answer if you decide another answer is more accurate; do not erase until you are ready to hand your paper in
      12. Answer all questions; guess unless instructed otherwise
      13. Leave time for review

   b. Essay questions
      1. Read each question carefully
      2. Determine exactly what is wanted. Underline key words or phrases.
      3. Decide on outline or paragraph answer

4. Include many different points and elements unless asked to develop any one or two points or elements
5. Show impartiality by giving pros and cons unless directed to select one side only
6. Make and write down any assumptions you find necessary to answer the questions
7. Watch your English, grammar, punctuation and choice of words
8. Time your answers; don't crowd material

8) Answering the essay question

Most essay questions can be answered by framing the specific response around several key words or ideas. Here are a few such key words or ideas:

M's: manpower, materials, methods, money, management
P's: purpose, program, policy, plan, procedure, practice, problems, pitfalls, personnel, public relations
    a. Six basic steps in handling problems:
        1. Preliminary plan and background development
        2. Collect information, data and facts
        3. Analyze and interpret information, data and facts
        4. Analyze and develop solutions as well as make recommendations
        5. Prepare report and sell recommendations
        6. Install recommendations and follow up effectiveness

    b. Pitfalls to avoid
        1. *Taking things for granted* – A statement of the situation does not necessarily imply that each of the elements is necessarily true; for example, a complaint may be invalid and biased so that all that can be taken for granted is that a complaint has been registered
        2. *Considering only one side of a situation* – Wherever possible, indicate several alternatives and then point out the reasons you selected the best one
        3. *Failing to indicate follow up* – Whenever your answer indicates action on your part, make certain that you will take proper follow-up action to see how successful your recommendations, procedures or actions turn out to be
        4. *Taking too long in answering any single question* – Remember to time your answers properly

IX. AFTER THE TEST

Scoring procedures differ in detail among civil service jurisdictions although the general principles are the same. Whether the papers are hand-scored or graded by machine we have described, they are nearly always graded by number. That is, the person who marks the paper knows only the number – never the name – of the applicant. Not until all the papers have been graded will they be matched with names. If other tests, such as training and experience or oral interview ratings have been given, scores will be combined. Different parts of the examination usually have different weights. For example, the written test might count 60 percent of the final grade, and a rating of training and experience 40 percent. In many jurisdictions, veterans will have a certain number of points added to their grades.

After the final grade has been determined, the names are placed in grade order and an eligible list is established. There are various methods for resolving ties between those who get the same final grade – probably the most common is to place first the name of the person whose application was received first. Job offers are made from the eligible list in the order the names appear on it. You will be notified of your grade and your rank as soon as all these computations have been made. This will be done as rapidly as possible.

People who are found to meet the requirements in the announcement are called "eligibles." Their names are put on a list of eligible candidates. An eligible's chances of getting a job depend on how high he stands on this list and how fast agencies are filling jobs from the list.

When a job is to be filled from a list of eligibles, the agency asks for the names of people on the list of eligibles for that job. When the civil service commission receives this request, it sends to the agency the names of the three people highest on this list. Or, if the job to be filled has specialized requirements, the office sends the agency the names of the top three persons who meet these requirements from the general list.

The appointing officer makes a choice from among the three people whose names were sent to him. If the selected person accepts the appointment, the names of the others are put back on the list to be considered for future openings.

That is the rule in hiring from all kinds of eligible lists, whether they are for typist, carpenter, chemist, or something else. For every vacancy, the appointing officer has his choice of any one of the top three eligibles on the list. This explains why the person whose name is on top of the list sometimes does not get an appointment when some of the persons lower on the list do. If the appointing officer chooses the second or third eligible, the No. 1 eligible does not get a job at once, but stays on the list until he is appointed or the list is terminated.

X. HOW TO PASS THE INTERVIEW TEST

The examination for which you applied requires an oral interview test. You have already taken the written test and you are now being called for the interview test – the final part of the formal examination.

You may think that it is not possible to prepare for an interview test and that there are no procedures to follow during an interview. Our purpose is to point out some things you can do in advance that will help you and some good rules to follow and pitfalls to avoid while you are being interviewed.

What is an interview supposed to test?

The written examination is designed to test the technical knowledge and competence of the candidate; the oral is designed to evaluate intangible qualities, not readily measured otherwise, and to establish a list showing the relative fitness of each candidate – as measured against his competitors – for the position sought. Scoring is not on the basis of "right" and "wrong," but on a sliding scale of values ranging from "not passable" to "outstanding." As a matter of fact, it is possible to achieve a relatively low score without a single "incorrect" answer because of evident weakness in the qualities being measured.

Occasionally, an examination may consist entirely of an oral test – either an individual or a group oral. In such cases, information is sought concerning the technical knowledges and abilities of the candidate, since there has been no written examination for this purpose. More commonly, however, an oral test is used to supplement a written examination.

Who conducts interviews?

The composition of oral boards varies among different jurisdictions. In nearly all, a representative of the personnel department serves as chairman. One of the members of the board may be a representative of the department in which the candidate would work. In some cases, "outside experts" are used, and, frequently, a businessman or some other representative of the general public is asked to serve. Labor and management or other special groups may be represented. The aim is to secure the services of experts in the appropriate field.

However the board is composed, it is a good idea (and not at all improper or unethical) to ascertain in advance of the interview who the members are and what groups they represent. When you are introduced to them, you will have some idea of their backgrounds and interests, and at least you will not stutter and stammer over their names.

What should be done before the interview?

While knowledge about the board members is useful and takes some of the surprise element out of the interview, there is other preparation which is more substantive. It *is* possible to prepare for an oral interview – in several ways:

1) Keep a copy of your application and review it carefully before the interview

This may be the only document before the oral board, and the starting point of the interview. Know what education and experience you have listed there, and the sequence and dates of all of it. Sometimes the board will ask you to review the highlights of your experience for them; you should not have to hem and haw doing it.

2) Study the class specification and the examination announcement

Usually, the oral board has one or both of these to guide them. The qualities, characteristics or knowledges required by the position sought are stated in these documents. They offer valuable clues as to the nature of the oral interview. For example, if the job involves supervisory responsibilities, the announcement will usually indicate that knowledge of modern supervisory methods and the qualifications of the candidate as a supervisor will be tested. If so, you can expect such questions, frequently in the form of a hypothetical situation which you are expected to solve. NEVER go into an oral without knowledge of the duties and responsibilities of the job you seek.

3) Think through each qualification required

Try to visualize the kind of questions you would ask if you were a board member. How well could you answer them? Try especially to appraise your own knowledge and background in each area, *measured against the job sought*, and identify any areas in which you are weak. Be critical and realistic – do not flatter yourself.

4) Do some general reading in areas in which you feel you may be weak

For example, if the job involves supervision and your past experience has NOT, some general reading in supervisory methods and practices, particularly in the field of human relations, might be useful. Do NOT study agency procedures or detailed manuals. The oral board will be testing your understanding and capacity, not your memory.

5) Get a good night's sleep and watch your general health and mental attitude

You will want a clear head at the interview. Take care of a cold or any other minor ailment, and of course, no hangovers.

What should be done on the day of the interview?

Now comes the day of the interview itself. Give yourself plenty of time to get there. Plan to arrive somewhat ahead of the scheduled time, particularly if your appointment is in the fore part of the day. If a previous candidate fails to appear, the board might be ready for you a bit early. By early afternoon an oral board is almost invariably behind schedule if there are many candidates, and you may have to wait. Take along a book or magazine to read, or your application to review, but leave any extraneous material in the waiting room when you go in for your interview. In any event, relax and compose yourself.

The matter of dress is important. The board is forming impressions about you – from your experience, your manners, your attitude, and your appearance. Give your personal appearance careful attention. Dress your best, but not your flashiest. Choose conservative, appropriate clothing, and be sure it is immaculate. This is a business interview, and your appearance should indicate that you regard it as such. Besides, being well groomed and properly dressed will help boost your confidence.

Sooner or later, someone will call your name and escort you into the interview room. *This is it.* From here on you are on your own. It is too late for any more preparation. But remember, you asked for this opportunity to prove your fitness, and you are here because your request was granted.

What happens when you go in?

The usual sequence of events will be as follows: The clerk (who is often the board stenographer) will introduce you to the chairman of the oral board, who will introduce you to the other members of the board. Acknowledge the introductions before you sit down. Do not be surprised if you find a microphone facing you or a stenotypist sitting by. Oral interviews are usually recorded in the event of an appeal or other review.

Usually the chairman of the board will open the interview by reviewing the highlights of your education and work experience from your application – primarily for the benefit of the other members of the board, as well as to get the material into the record. Do not interrupt or comment unless there is an error or significant misinterpretation; if that is the case, do not hesitate. But do not quibble about insignificant matters. Also, he will usually ask you some question about your education, experience or your present job – partly to get you to start talking and to establish the interviewing "rapport." He may start the actual questioning, or turn it over to one of the other members. Frequently, each member undertakes the questioning on a particular area, one in which he is perhaps most competent, so you can expect each member to participate in the examination. Because time is limited, you may also expect some rather abrupt switches in the direction the questioning takes, so do not be upset by it. Normally, a board member will not pursue a single line of questioning unless he discovers a particular strength or weakness.

After each member has participated, the chairman will usually ask whether any member has any further questions, then will ask you if you have anything you wish to add. Unless you are expecting this question, it may floor you. Worse, it may start you off on an extended, extemporaneous speech. The board is not usually seeking more information. The question is principally to offer you a last opportunity to present further qualifications or to indicate that you have nothing to add. So, if you feel that a significant qualification or characteristic has been overlooked, it is proper to point it out in a sentence or so. Do not compliment the board on the thoroughness of their examination – they have been sketchy, and you know it. If you wish, merely say, "No thank you, I have nothing further to add." This is a point where you can "talk yourself out" of a good impression or fail to present an important bit of information. Remember, *you close the interview yourself.*

The chairman will then say, "That is all, Mr. _____, thank you." Do not be startled; the interview is over, and quicker than you think. Thank him, gather your belongings and take your leave. Save your sigh of relief for the other side of the door.

How to put your best foot forward

Throughout this entire process, you may feel that the board individually and collectively is trying to pierce your defenses, seek out your hidden weaknesses and embarrass and confuse you. Actually, this is not true. They are obliged to make an appraisal of your qualifications for the job you are seeking, and they want to see you in your best light. Remember, they must interview all candidates and a non-cooperative candidate may become a failure in spite of their best efforts to bring out his qualifications. Here are 15 suggestions that will help you:

1) Be natural – Keep your attitude confident, not cocky

If you are not confident that you can do the job, do not expect the board to be. Do not apologize for your weaknesses, try to bring out your strong points. The board is interested in a positive, not negative, presentation. Cockiness will antagonize any board member and make him wonder if you are covering up a weakness by a false show of strength.

2) Get comfortable, but don't lounge or sprawl

Sit erectly but not stiffly. A careless posture may lead the board to conclude that you are careless in other things, or at least that you are not impressed by the importance of the occasion. Either conclusion is natural, even if incorrect. Do not fuss with your clothing, a pencil or an ashtray. Your hands may occasionally be useful to emphasize a point; do not let them become a point of distraction.

3) Do not wisecrack or make small talk

This is a serious situation, and your attitude should show that you consider it as such. Further, the time of the board is limited – they do not want to waste it, and neither should you.

4) Do not exaggerate your experience or abilities

In the first place, from information in the application or other interviews and sources, the board may know more about you than you think. Secondly, you probably will not get away with it. An experienced board is rather adept at spotting such a situation, so do not take the chance.

5) If you know a board member, do not make a point of it, yet do not hide it

Certainly you are not fooling him, and probably not the other members of the board. Do not try to take advantage of your acquaintanceship – it will probably do you little good.

6) Do not dominate the interview

Let the board do that. They will give you the clues – do not assume that you have to do all the talking. Realize that the board has a number of questions to ask you, and do not try to take up all the interview time by showing off your extensive knowledge of the answer to the first one.

7) Be attentive

You only have 20 minutes or so, and you should keep your attention at its sharpest throughout. When a member is addressing a problem or question to you, give him your undivided attention. Address your reply principally to him, but do not exclude the other board members.

8) Do not interrupt

A board member may be stating a problem for you to analyze. He will ask you a question when the time comes. Let him state the problem, and wait for the question.

9) Make sure you understand the question

Do not try to answer until you are sure what the question is. If it is not clear, restate it in your own words or ask the board member to clarify it for you. However, do not haggle about minor elements.

10) Reply promptly but not hastily

A common entry on oral board rating sheets is "candidate responded readily," or "candidate hesitated in replies." Respond as promptly and quickly as you can, but do not jump to a hasty, ill-considered answer.

11) Do not be peremptory in your answers

A brief answer is proper – but do not fire your answer back. That is a losing game from your point of view. The board member can probably ask questions much faster than you can answer them.

12) Do not try to create the answer you think the board member wants

He is interested in what kind of mind you have and how it works – not in playing games. Furthermore, he can usually spot this practice and will actually grade you down on it.

13) Do not switch sides in your reply merely to agree with a board member

Frequently, a member will take a contrary position merely to draw you out and to see if you are willing and able to defend your point of view. Do not start a debate, yet do not surrender a good position. If a position is worth taking, it is worth defending.

14) Do not be afraid to admit an error in judgment if you are shown to be wrong

The board knows that you are forced to reply without any opportunity for careful consideration. Your answer may be demonstrably wrong. If so, admit it and get on with the interview.

15) Do not dwell at length on your present job

The opening question may relate to your present assignment. Answer the question but do not go into an extended discussion. You are being examined for a *new* job, not your present one. As a matter of fact, try to phrase ALL your answers in terms of the job for which you are being examined.

Basis of Rating

Probably you will forget most of these "do's" and "don'ts" when you walk into the oral interview room. Even remembering them all will not ensure you a passing grade. Perhaps you did not have the qualifications in the first place. But remembering them will help you to put your best foot forward, without treading on the toes of the board members.

Rumor and popular opinion to the contrary notwithstanding, an oral board wants you to make the best appearance possible. They know you are under pressure – but they also want to see how you respond to it as a guide to what your reaction would be under the pressures of the job you seek. They will be influenced by the degree of poise you display, the personal traits you show and the manner in which you respond.

ABOUT THIS BOOK

This book contains tests divided into Examination Sections. Go through each test, answering every question in the margin. At the end of each test look at the answer key and check your answers. On the ones you got wrong, look at the right answer choice and learn. Do not fill in the answers first. Do not memorize the questions and answers, but understand the answer and principles involved. On your test, the questions will likely be different from the samples. Questions are changed and new ones added. If you understand these past questions you should have success with any changes that arise. Tests may consist of several types of questions. We have additional books on each subject should more study be advisable or necessary for you. Finally, the more you study, the better prepared you will be. This book is intended to be the last thing you study before you walk into the examination room. Prior study of relevant texts is also recommended. NLC publishes some of these in our Fundamental Series. Knowledge and good sense are important factors in passing your exam. Good luck also helps. So now study this Passbook, absorb the material contained within and take that knowledge into the examination. Then do your best to pass that exam.

———

EXAMINATION SECTION

EXAMINATION SECTION
TEST 1

DIRECTIONS: Each question or incomplete statement is followed by several suggested answers or completions. Select the one that BEST answers the question or completes the statement. *PRINT THE LETTEE OF THE CORRECT ANSWER IN THE SPACE AT THE RIGHT.*

1. An AC circuit consists only of a pure inductance and a power source.
   The relationship between the voltage and the current in this circuit is that the   1.____

   A. voltage lags the current
   B. current leads the voltage
   C. current lags the voltage
   D. voltage and current are in phase

2. The power factor of a load is equal to the _____ power divided by the _____ power.   2.____

   A. apparent; true   B. true; apparent
   C. reactive; apparent   D. apparent; reactive

3. A 10-ohm and a 20-ohm resistor are connected in parallel.   3.____
   The total line current drawn by this parallel combination is 30 amps.
   Under these conditions, the line voltage will be _____ volts.

   A. 150   B. 200   C. 300   D. 600

4. A 20-ohm resistor is connected in series with a parallel combination of two resistors, one   4.____
   of which is 10 ohms, the other 40 ohms.
   If the voltage across the parallel combination is 40 volts, the voltage across the 20-ohm series resistor is _____ volts.

   A. 20   B. 40   C. 80   D. 100

5. A certain 120-volt single-phase AC circuit has a power factor of 80 percent and a watt-   5.____
   meter reading of 1150 watts. The current drawn by the circuit is _____ amperes.

   A. 8   B. 10   C. 12   D. 14

6. If the voltage between lines of a 3-phase, 3-wire delta connected system is 2400 volts,   6.____
   then the phase voltage is _____ volts.

   A. 2400   B. 2080   C. 1380   D. 1200

7. A circuit consists of an inductive reactance of 15 ohms and a resistor of 20 ohms in   7.____
   series across a 100-volt, 60 cycle AC supply.
   The current in this circuit is _____ amperes.

   A. 2.9   B. 4.0   C. 5.8   D. 8.0

8. A 3-phase, 3-wire, 208-volt, 60-cycle AC service supplies a balanced load consisting of   8.____
   three 30-ohm resistors connected in wye.
   The line current under these conditions is MOST NEARLY _____ amperes.

   A. 3.5   B. 4.0   C. 6.9   D. 8.0

1

9. If the level of the electrolyte in a lead-acid storage battery falls below the top of the plates   9.____
because of evaporation under normal operating conditions, it is BEST to add

    A. electrolyte   B. sulphuric acid
    C. hydrochloric acid   D. water

10. A 600-volt cartridge fuse must have knife blade contacts if its current rating exceeds   10.____
_____ amperes.

    A. 30   B. 60   C. 80   D. 100

11. When the magnitude of the short circuit currents in a feeder circuit must be limited, this is   11.____
USUALLY accomplished by means of

    A. resistors   B. reactors
    C. capacitors   D. contactors

12. The cross-sectional area in circular mils of a stranded cable having 37 strands, each of   12.____
which has a diameter of 90 nils, is MOST NEARLY

    A. 81,000   B. 95,000   C. 300,000   D. 942,000

13. A coil having an average diameter of 4 inches is to be made up from a 1,260-ft.-long   13.____
length of wire.
The number of turns in this coil will be MOST NEARLY

    A. 100   B. 315   C. 1,200   D. 3,780

14. The device commonly known as a *growler* is FREQUENTLY used to   14.____

    A. test DC armature windings for shorts
    B. clean commutators
    C. check insulation of circuit wiring within a raceway
    D. sound alarms

15. When a megger is applied alternately to the two leads of a direct-current electrolytic   15.____
capacitor, the readings will

    A. start and remain at zero for both connections
    B. start at zero but increase gradually for one of the connections
    C. start at zero but increase gradually for both connections
    D. be high at first but decrease gradually for both connections

16. The devices used to convert direct current to alternating current are called   16.____

    A. rectifiers   B. transformers
    C. rotary converters   D. inverters

17. Of the following conditions, the one which is MOST likely to cause flashing or excessive   17.____
arcing from brush to brush in a motor is

    A. brushes being set at the improper angle for the direction of rotation
    B. brush pressure being too great
    C. brushes being too hard
    D. excessively high voltage on the line

18. The currents in the armature equalizer connections in a DC generator are

    A. passed through the brushes
    B. pure DC currents
    C. DC currents containing 120 cycle ripple
    D. alternating currents

18.____

19. A generating station has one 1000-Kw and two 2000-Kw generators.
To supply 2000 Kw MOST economically, the operating conditions should be

    A. two 2000-Kw generators at half load
    B. one 2000-Kw generator at full load
    C. the 1000-Kw generator at full load and one 2000-Kw generator at half load
    D. the 1000-Kw generator at full load and each of the 2000-Kw generators at 500-Kw load

19.____

20. The terminal voltage of a DC shunt generator having an armature current of 100 amperes, an armature resistance of 0.02 ohms, and a generated E.M.F. of 222 volts is MOST NEARLY _____ volts.

    A. 200   B. 220   C. 224   D. 242

20.____

21. The number of poles in the field of an alternator generating voltage at a frequency of 60 cycles per second while rotating at 1200 r.p.m. is

    A. 4   B. 6   C. 8   D. 12

21.____

22. If the field of a shunt motor opens while running, the motor will

    A. stop running
    B. continue to run at the same speed
    C. slow down
    D. run away

22.____

23. To reverse the direction of rotation of a cumulative compound motor, and not have it run as a differential compound motor, reverse the connections to the _____ field.

    A. shunt   B. series
    C. shunt field and to the series   D. armature and to the shunt

23.____

24. The MAIN contributing factor to motor stator failure *usually* is

    A. eddy currents   B. bearing trouble
    C. dirt   D. hysteresis

24.____

25. The input of a motor is 40,000 watts and its efficiency is 80 percent.
The TOTAL energy loss is_____ watts.

    A. 32,000   B. 8,000   C. 5,000   D. 2,500

25.____

26. The full load current of a three-phase 5 hp motor operating at 200 volts, 60 cycles, and having an efficiency of 80 percent and a power factor of 85 percent is MOST NEARLY _____ amperes.

    A. 9.7   B. 12.1   C. 14.4   D. 18.0

26.____

27. Of the following motors, the one that has the BEST speed regulation is the _____ motor.   27._____

    A. series   B. compound
    C. shunt   D. split-phase

28. The full load speed of a 60-cycle, 208-volt, 3-phase induction motor having 6 poles and operating with a slip of 10% is MOST NEARLY _____ r.p.m.   28._____

    A. 540   B. 600   C. 1080   D. 1200

29. Of the following, a MAJOR advantage of an AC synchronous motor is that it(s)   29._____

    A. does not require direct current
    B. can be used for power factor correction
    C. speed of rotation can be varied by means of a field rheostat
    D. can respond to disturbances in the power system by hunting

30. If the field current of a synchronous motor is increased to a point which makes the synchronous motor overexcited, the   30._____

    A. power factor will be decreased
    B. motor rotational speed will be increased
    C. motor rotational speed will be decreased
    D. motor will take a leading current

31. When transformers are to be operated in parallel, it is NOT necessary that the transformer have the same   31._____

    A. ratio of transformation
    B. voltage rating
    C. polarity of the terminals that connect together
    D. KVA rating

32. A transformer rated at 200 KVA is FULLY loaded with a lagging power factor of 80% when it is supplying   32._____

    A. 160 KW   B. 200 KW   C. 250 KVA   D. 80 KVA

33. If the current in the primary of a current transformer is 500 amperes and the transformer has a ratio of 100 to 5, an ammeter connected to the secondary will read MOST NEARLY _____ amperes.   33._____

    A. 5   B. 20   C. 25   D. 100

34. Assume that a switchboard ammeter which is connected to a current transformer is damaged and must be removed without interrupting the service.
Of the following, an ESSENTIAL precaution to be taken before disconnecting the ammeter is to   34._____

    A. ground the mid-point of the transformer secondary
    B. ground one end of the transformer secondary
    C. disconnect both ammeter leads simultaneously
    D. short the secondary of the transformer

35. A DC relay is rated at 6 volts and 120 ohms.
This relay can be operated from a 120 volt line by connecting a _____ -ohm resistance in _____ with the relay.

    A. 2280; parallel   B. 2280; series
    C. 2400; parallel   D. 2400; series

35._____

36. Some relays are provided with dash-pots.
The FUNCTION of these dash-pots is to provide

    A. delayed time action   B. instantaneous time action
    C. undervoltage protection   D. overcurrent protection

36._____

37. An ammeter has a full scale deflection for a current of 0.01 amperes and an internal resistance of 20 ohms.
In order to have the ammeter read full-scale for a current of 10 amperes and not damage its movement, a shunt should be used having a value of _____ ohms.

    A. 10   B. 0.2   C. 0.02   D. 0.01

37._____

38. An air circuit breaker has contacts that flash. The MOST probable cause of this trouble is that the

    A. overload relays are set too low
    B. contacts are overheating
    C. closing-coil circuit is defective
    D. barriers are broken

38._____

39. The MAIN purpose of a *shunt trip* on a circuit breaker is to

    A. open all phases in a polyphase circuit if there is a failure in any one of the phases
    B. prevent phase reversal
    C. permit the breaker to be opened electrically from a remote location, regardless of load conditions at the breaker
    D. prevent manual tripping

39._____

40. The grid-controlled gas-type electronic tube MOST often used in motor control circuits is the

    A. magnetron   B. thyratron
    C. ignitron   D. strobatron

40._____

KEY (CORRECT ANSWERS)

1.	C	11.	B	21.	B	31.	D
2.	B	12.	C	22.	D	32.	A
3.	B	13.	C	23.	C	33.	C
4.	D	14.	A	24.	C	34.	D
5.	C	15.	B	25.	B	35.	B
6.	A	16.	D	26.	C	36.	A
7.	B	17.	D	27.	C	37.	C
8.	C	18.	D	28.	C	38.	D
9.	D	19.	B	29.	B	39.	C
10.	B	20.	B	30.	D	40.	B

———

TEST 2

DIRECTIONS: Each question or incomplete statement is followed by several suggested answers or completions. Select the one that BEST answers the question or completes the statement. *PRINT THE LETTER OF THE CORRECT ANSWER IN THE SPACE AT THE RIGHT.*

1. Under normal atmospheric conditions, a pressure gauge that reads 24 inches of mercury is indicating an *absolute pressure* of MOST NEARLY _____ P.S.I.

    A. 26.5   B. 14.7   C. 11.8   D. 8.7

1._____

2. The PRIMARY function of a hygrometer is to measure

    A. relative humidity   B. specific gravity
    C. liquid levels   D. pressure differentials

2._____

3. A venturi meter is used to measure the rate of

    A. vibration of engine footings
    B. electric power consumption
    C. heat transfer
    D. fluid flow

3._____

4. The PRINCIPAL thickening agent used in lubricating greases is

    A. metallic soap   B. olein
    C. palmitin   D. lecithin

4._____

5. The specific gravity of liquids is USUALLY determined by means of a

    A. bolometer   B. calorimeter
    C. fathometer   D. hydrometer

5._____

6. The pull required on the fall line (neglecting friction) to hoist a 120-pound weight, using a four-part block and tackle, is _____ lbs.

    A. 30   B. 60   C. 80   D. 100

6._____

7. Of the following terms, the one which does NOT describe a way of finishing the ends of a rope is the

    A. eye splice   B. backlash
    C. whip   D. bight

7._____

8. When hoisting a load by means of a sling, the stress in each leg of the sling will

    A. increase as the angle between the horizontal and the sling leg decreases
    B. decrease as the angle between the horizontal and the sling leg decreases
    C. increase as the angle between the horizontal and the sling leg increases
    D. be independent of the angle between the horizontal and the sling leg

8._____

9. The MAXIMUM pressure in an upright cylinder 6 feet in diameter, 8 feet high, and open at the top, when filled to the brim with water, is MOST NEARLY _____ lbs/sq.ft.

    A. 250   B. 375   C. 500   D. 750

9._____

10. The MAXIMUM height to which water can be lifted by means of suction alone, at sea level, is APPROXIMATELY _____ feet.

    A. 10   B. 22   C. 34   D. 47

10.____

11. The TOTAL number of 4-inch diameter pipes that is required to equal the water flow capacity of an 8-inch diarieter pipe (neglecting friction) is

    A. 2   B. 3   C. 4   D. 5

11.____

12. The number of threads, per inch, on the standard machine screw MOST suitable for general use is

    A. 50   B. 32   C. 17   D. 10

12.____

13. The friction losses which occur when water flows through a pipe vary MOST NEARLY _____ with the _____ .

    A. *directly*; velocity squared
    B. *inversely*; velocity squared
    C. *directly*; velocity
    D. *inversely*; velocity

13.____

14. Small by-pass lines are sometimes furnished around large gate valves MAINLY to

    A. balance the pressure on the gate when the valve is being opened
    B. permit dumping of the excess fluid
    C. meter the flow
    D. divert fluid in case the valve becomes stuck

14.____

15. The sudden surge caused by an abrupt change in the speed of the pumps in a closed liquid piping system is USUALLY called

    A. tailing   B. water hammer
    C. precipitation   D. jetting

15.____

16. The valve that permits water to flow in one direction only is the _____ valve.

    A. gate   B. globe   C. angle   D. check

16.____

17. Most flanged butterfly valves can be brought from a fully closed position to a fully opened position in _____ turn(s).

    A. two full   B. one full
    C. a half   D. a quarter

17.____

18. The efficiency of two centrifugal pumps operating in parallel is _____ of one of the pumps operating alone.

    A. one-half that
    B. practically the same as that
    C. twice that
    D. four times that

18.____

19. Assume that a spur gear having 20 teeth revolves at 80 r.p.m. and drives another spur gear having 40 teeth. The speed at which the gear having 40 teeth revolves is _____ r.p.m.

    A. 160   B. 40   C. 20   D. 10

19._____

20. A centrifugal pump has a plain flat-joint seal between the impeller and the casing. If the clearance of the seal becomes enlarged due to wear, thereby reducing the pump's efficiency, it would be GOOD practice to

    A. tighten down on the casing
    B. use the pumps only in an emergency
    C. replace the wearing ring
    D. renew the impeller

20._____

21. The one of the following statements which CORRECTLY describes a speed characteristic for a centrifugal pump under normal operating conditions is:

    A. Capacity varies directly with the square of the speed
    B. Total head varies directly with the square of the speed
    C. Fluid power varies directly with the square of the speed
    D. Fluid power varies directly with the speed

21._____

22. The MAIN function of a pump stuffing box is to

    A. protect the pump against leakage at the point where the shaft passes through the pump casing
    B. provide a ball bearing race
    C. couple the pump to its motor
    D. prime the pump

22._____

23. The PROPER order of the events that take place in a 4-stroke internal combustion engine is:

    A. Air intake, power expansion, compression, and exhaust
    B. Power expansion, air intake, compression, and exhaust
    C. Air intake, compression, power expansion, and exhaust
    D.

23._____

24. The number of cycles in an internal combustion engine is AT LEAST _____ cycles.

    A. two   B. three   C. four   D. five

24._____

25. The lumens per watt taken by a lamp varies with the type and size of lamp. Given that a one candlepower light source emits 12.57 lumens, the lumens per watt taken by a 75 candlepower lamp drawing 40 watts is APPROXIMATELY

    A. 1.9   B. 6.7   C. 23.6   D. 240

25._____

26. A 230-volt, 25-cycle magnetic brake coil is to be rewound to operate properly on 60 cycles at the same voltage.
Assuming that the coil at 25-cycles has 1800 turns, at 60 cycles the number of turns should be

    A. reduced to 750   B. increased to 2400
    C. reduced to 420   D. increased to 3000

26._____

27. Nichrome wire having a resistance of 200 ohms per 100 feet is to be used for a heater   27.____
requiring a total resistance of 10 ohms.
The length, in feet, of wire required is

    A. 5   B. 15   C. 25   D. 50

28. The MAIN reason for grounding conduit is to prevent the conduit from becoming   28.____

    A. corroded by electrolysis
    B. magnetized
    C. a source of radio interference
    D. accidentally energized at a higher potential than ground

29. A feeder consisting of a positive and a negative wire supplies a motor load. The feeder is   29.____
connected to bus-bars having a constant potential of 230 volts. The feeder is 500 ft. long
and consists of two 250,000 circular-mil conductors. The maximum load on the feeder is
170 amps. Assume that the resistance of 1000 ft. of this cable is 0.0431 ohm.
The voltage, at the motor terminals, is MOST NEARLY

    A. 201V   B. 209V   C. 213V   D. 217V

30. With reference to Question 29, the efficiency of transmission, in percent, is MOST   30.____
NEARLY

    A. 83%   B. 87%   C. 91%   D. 97%

31. With reference to AC motors, in addition to overload, many other things cause fuses to   31.____
blow.
The fuse will blow if, in starting an AC motor, the operator throws the starting switch of
the compensator to the running position

    A. too slowly
    B. too quickly
    C. with main switch in open position
    D. with main switch in closed position

32. A change in speed of a DC motor of 10 to 15 percent can USUALLY be made by   32.____

    A. rewinding the armature
    B. rewinding the field
    C. decreasing the number of turns in the field coils
    D. increasing or decreasing the gap between the armature and field

33. Of the following types of fire extinguishers, the one MOST suitable for use on fires in   33.____
electrical equipment is the _____ extinguisher.

    A. soda-acid   B. loaded stream
    C. foam   D. dry chemical

34. Portable fire extinguishers suitable for use on electrical fires are USUALLY identified by a   34.____
label with the following symbol_____ in a _____.

    A. *A*; triangle   B. *B*; square
    C. *C*; circle   D. *D*; five-pointed star

35. When flammable liquids are poured from one container to another, a bond wire is some- 35.____
    times connected between the containers to

    A. prevent the liquid from spilling
    B. prevent the containers from dropping
    C. ensure that the containers will be sealed after pouring is completed
    D. eliminate sparks due to static electricity

36. The proper way to lift a heavy object includes all of the following techniques EXCEPT 36.____

    A. placing the feet as far away from the object as possible
    B. bending the knees
    C. keeping the back straight
    D. lifting with the arm and leg muscles

37. The contents of different piping systems are sometimes identified by means of standard 37.____
    color codes, such as the one recommended by the American National Standards Insti-
    tute (formerly the American Standards Institute). According to this Institute's standards, a
    piping system used for fire protection should be designated by the color

    A. green   B. blue   C. red   D. yellow

38. Assume that the contents of a container are described as *TOXIC*. 38.____
    This means they are

    A. explosive   B. fragile
    C. poisonous   D. volatile

39. An authoritative source of emergency information on antidotes is the 39.____

    A. Fire Department
    B. Poison Control Center, Department of Health
    C. public library
    D. National Labor Relations Board

40. Unexpected operation of electrical equipment that can be started by remote control may 40.____
    cause injury to workers making repairs.
    Before making repairs on such equipment, it is GOOD practice to

    A. follow a lockout procedure
    B. bypass the interlocks
    C. ground all live conductors
    D. uncouple all motors

KEY (CORRECT ANSWERS)

1.	A	11.	C	21.	B	31.	B
2.	A	12.	B	22.	A	32.	D
3.	D	13.	A	23.	C	33.	D
4.	A	14.	A	24.	A	34.	C
5.	D	15.	B	25.	C	35.	D
6.	A	16.	D	26.	A	36.	A
7.	D	17.	D	27.	D	37.	C
8.	A	18.	B	28.	D	38.	C
9.	C	19.	B	29.	D	39.	B
10.	C	20.	D	30.	D	40.	A

————

EXAMINATION SECTION
TEST 1

DIRECTIONS: Each question or incomplete statement is followed by several suggested answers or completions. Select the one that BEST answers the question or completes the statement. *PRINT THE LETTER OF THE CORRECT ANSWER IN THE SPACE AT THE RIGHT.*

1. Assume that one of the men under your supervision asks you a technical question to which you do not know the answer.
    Of the following, it is BEST that you

    A. tell him that you do not know the answer but that you will get the information for him
    B. tell him to find out for himself
    C. bluff him by giving him an answer
    D. pretend that you are needed elsewhere urgently and avoid giving an answer

    1._____

2. In ordering standard cartridge fuses, it is necessary to specify only the

    A. voltage of the circuit
    B. current capacity of the circuit and the power to be dissipated
    C. power to be dissipated
    D. current capacity and the voltage of the circuit

    2._____

3. A synchronous motor having 12 poles and operating on 60-cycle alternating current would have a speed, in r.p.m., of MOST NEARLY

    A. 300   B. 360   C. 600   D. 720

    3._____

4. In a fully charged lead acid storage battery, the active material of the plates is

    A. lead peroxide on the positive and sponge lead on the negative plates
    B. lead peroxide on the positive and the negative plates
    C. sponge lead on the positive and the negative plates
    D. lead peroxide on the negative and sponge lead on the positive plates

    4._____

5. Assume that a three-phase wound rotor induction motor is running at full speed and no load when the connection between the windings and one of the collector rings suddenly breaks.
    Under this condition, the motor will

    A. immediately stop
    B. continue to run at full speed but will slow down when the load is added
    C. continue to run at full speed but will overheat
    D. run at half speed

    5._____

6. Of the following, the PRIMARY function of a pyrometer is to measure

    A. revolutions per minute   B. synchronization
    C. gallons per minute   D. temperature

    6._____

7. In general, the temperature of a gas or vapor compressed in a limited space will

    A. increase
    B. decrease

    7._____

13

C.   decrease and then gradually increase
D.   remain the same

8.   Assume that the stem of a large valve has multiple threads. Of the following, the BEST   8._____
reason for using multiple threads in this instance is to

A.   decrease the length of travel of the stem
B.   permit the valve to be opened or closed faster
C.   reduce the friction due to corrosion
D.   prevent backlash

9.   Of the following, the valve generally used where accurate throttling is required such as   9._____
for instrument, gage, or meter line service is the _____ valve.

A.   butterfly   B.   globe
C.   needle   D.   O.S. and Y.

10.   Of the following, the one which is NOT part of a safe, well-planned, lockout procedure is   10._____

A.   no two locks should be the same
B.   furnish all plant personnel with identical padlocks and keys
C.   each key should fit only one lock
D.   duplicate sets of keys not to be readily accessible to the worker in case a key is lost

11.   Of the following, the one which shows the BEST supervisory conduct is   11._____

A.   assume credit for a subordinate's ideas
B.   admit your mistakes
C.   never be friendly with your subordinates
D.   gain respect by losing your temper occasionally

12.   Of the following, the BEST practical way to keep morale high among the men/women he   12._____
supervises is to

A.   individually assist the men/women on all of their jobs
B.   praise the men/women when they do a good job
C.   reward good work with special privileges
D.   give good workers the best jobs

13.   Of the following, the BEST procedure to use when it becomes necessary to reprimand a   13._____
worker is to

A.   reprimand him in private rather than in public, even if you must wait a day
B.   avoid speaking directly about the problem so as not to insult the worker
C.   be fair and give the identical reprimand to all workers rather than change it to suit
the individual involved
D.   always reprimand the worker immediately to prevent others from making the same
mistake

14.   Assume that you have told one of your men how to do a certain job. While you are   14._____
absent, your supervisor checks on the job and gives this man different orders.
Of the following, it would be BEST for you to

A.   talk the matter over with your boss privately
B.   tell the man that he should have told the supervisor to see you first

C. always check with your supervisor in the future before issuing orders
D. tell your men to always follow your orders without change

15. You feel that the morale of your crew would improve if they were permitted to demon-   15.____
strate their skills and prove their ability.
Of the following, the condition under which it is LEAST likely that you will achieve this
goal is if they

    A. all have similar skills
    B. are frequently trained to use new equipment and learn new techniques
    C. are closely supervised
    D. are required to do relatively complex tasks using their own initiative

16. Of the following, the MOST important step in the process of training a worker to perform   16.____
a new task is

    A. explain what to do and how to do it
    B. show what to do and how to do it
    C. have the workers practice the task under supervision
    D. make sure the worker understands why he is doing it

17. Of the following, the one which is NOT a distinguishing feature of a *preventive* mainte-   17.____
nance program is

    A. periodic inspection to uncover potential trouble
    B. diligent adjustment and repair of minor troubles
    C. obtain and keep records of normal operating temperatures, pressures, etc., and
       investigate any changes
    D. make only those repairs necessary to get equipment back into service

18. The direction of rotation of a DC shunt motor can be reversed by reversing   18.____

    A. both the field and the armature connections
    B. either the field or the armature connections
    C. the line connections
    D. the residual field

19. The insulation on high voltage cables must be capable of resisting the gas sometimes   19.____
produced by electrical action in the vicinity of high voltage.
This gas is called

    A. freon   B. oxygen   C. neon   D. ozone

20. A 5-volt voltmeter has a resistance of 500 ohms.   20.____
Of the following resistances, the one which should be placed in series with this instrument in order to measure voltages up to 150 volts is _____ ohms.

    A. 75,000   B. 14,500   C. 2,500   D. 750

21. Assume that a certain 120-volt single-phase AC circuit draws a current of 12 amperes   21.____
and a wattmeter in the circuit reads 1150 watts.
The power factor, in percent, of this circuit is MOST NEARLY

    A. 75   B. 80   C. 85   D. 95

22. If the voltage between lines in a 3-phase, 4-wire system is 4160 volts, the voltage to neu-   22.____
tral is MOST NEARLY

   A. 2400   B. 2080   C. 1380   D. 1200

23. Assume that the contacts of an air circuit breaker flash from one to the other.   23.____
Of the following troubles, the one which is MOST likely to cause these symptoms is

   A. overload relays set low
   B. overheating
   C. closing coil circuit open
   D. barriers broken

24. The term *trip-free* applies to a circuit breaker that   24.____

   A. cannot be tripped when the operating lever is held in the closed position
   B. can be tripped only by the operator
   C. can be tripped by the overload mechanism even though the operating lever is held
       in the closed position
   D. is tripped from a shunt-circuit relay

25. The insulation resistance of a certain rubber-insulated single conductor cable 2200 feet   25.____
long is 360 megohms.
If a 1100-foot section of this cable is cut off, it will have an insulation resistance, in
megohms, of MOST NEARLY

   A. 1400   B. 720   C. 180   D. 90

26. When the level of the electrolyte in a lead-acid storage battery has fallen below the top of   26.____
the plates, the MOST preferred of the following actions is to raise the electrolyte level
_____ charging by adding _____.

   A. before; water   B. after; water
   C. before; sulfuric acid   D. after; sulfuric acid

27. The gases usually generated by electrolytic action while charging a lead-acid storage   27.____
battery are

   A. sulfur dioxide and lead sulphate
   B. hydrogen and chlorine
   C. hydrogen and oxygen
   D. chlorine and oxygen

28. On a DC generator, the polarity of an interpole is the same as that of the _____ in the   28.____
direction of rotation.

   A. interpole preceding it,   B. main pole it follows,
   C. main pole it precedes,   D. interpole following it,

29. The distance between the center lines of adjacent north and south poles, measured   29.____
along the circumference at the armature surface of an alternator, is called the

   A. stator pitch   B. pole circumference
   C. pole pitch   D. pitch factor

30. Compensator starters for polyphase squirrel cage motors are basically   30.____

    A. autotransformers
    B. resistance banks
    C. delta-wye switches
    D. QMQB across-the-line switches

31. In general, the power factor of a polyphase squirrel cage induction motor will   31.____

    A. increase if the load increases
    B. decrease if the load increases
    C. increase if the load decreases
    D. remain the same regardless of the load

32. A certain pumping station uses five large centrifugal pumps. Three are driven by wound   32.____
rotor induction motors, and two are driven by synchronous motors.
The MAIN reason for this combination is that

    A. wound rotor induction motors can be used to improve the power factor
    B. synchronous motors can be used to provide flexibility due to speed variation
    C. synchronous motors can be used to improve the power factor
    D. wound rotor induction motors are used because their speed is absolutely constant

33. Assume that the input of a certain motor is 32,000 watts and its losses are 4,000 watts.   33.____
The efficiency, in percent, of this motor is MOST NEARLY

    A. 88.8   B. 87.5   C. 81.3   D. 77.7

34. After repairs to the electrical supply, a three-phase, 3-wire, AC wound rotor induction   34.____
motor is found to rotate in the wrong direction.
In order to reverse the direction of rotation, it is necessary to

    A. reverse the field connections
    B. reverse any two supply lines connected to the stator
    C. reverse two leads connected to the rotor
    D. change the phase rotation of the rotor leads

35. Assume that several three-phase induction motors which are supplied through the same   35.____
oil circuit breaker all hum but will not start,
Of the following troubles, the one that is MOST likely to be responsible for such a situation is

    A. the fuse of one motor is blown
    B. one set of breaker contacts is so badly burned that they do not complete the con-
       nection
    C. all contacts of the circuit breaker are welded shut
    D. tripping mechanism of breaker is jammed so that trip coil pistons do not release
       toggle

36. In order to determine the no-load speed of a wound rotor induction motor, the load MUST   36.____
be disconnected and the motor run with

    A. resistance equal to the rotor resistance in series with the stator leads
    B. resistance equal to the stator resistance in the rotor

17

C. the rotor resistance all in
D. the rotor resistance short-circuited

37. Assume that a certain AC motor is started by means of a compensator. At times, although the motor is not overloaded, the fuse blows when the operator throws the compensator from the starting to the running position. Of the following, the action MOST likely to cause this trouble is that the operator throws the starting switch of the compensator to the running position

    37._____

    A. with the main switch closed
    B. too slowly
    C. too quickly
    D. with the main switch open

38. Of the following, the BEST use for a one-to-one transformer is to

    38._____

    A. electrically isolate the load from the source of supply
    B. connect voltmeters to high voltage circuits
    C. change from three-phase to two-phase
    D. connect voltmeters to low voltage circuits

39. Assume that an auto transformer draws 25 amperes from a 400-volt line in order to supply 100 amperes at 100 volts to a load.
The current flowing in that portion of the auto transformer winding across which the load is connected is _____ amperes.

    39._____

    A. 125   B. 75   C. 100   D. 20

40. Of the following, the MOST important precaution that should be observed in using a current instrument transformer is to

    40._____

    A. open the primary circuit after opening the secondary
    B. open the secondary circuit with the primary energized
    C. short circuit the primary after opening the secondary circuit
    D. short circuit the secondary prior to opening the secondary circuit

---

KEY (CORRECT ANSWERS)

1. A	11. B	21. B	31. A
2. D	12. B	22. A	32. C
3. C	13. A	23. D	33. B
4. A	14. A	24. C	34. B
5. D	15. C	25. B	35. B
6. D	16. C	26. A	36. D
7. A	17. D	27. C	37. C
8. B	18. B	28. B	38. A
9. C	19. D	29. C	39. B
10. B	20. B	30. A	40. D

TEST 2

DIRECTIONS: Each question or incomplete statement is followed by several suggested answers or completions. Select the one that BEST answers the question or completes the statement. *PRINT THE LETTER OF THE CORRECT ANSWER IN THE SPACE AT THE RIGHT.*

1. Assume that three single-phase transformers each have a primary rated at 2400 volts and a secondary rated at 480 volts.
   In order to obtain a 480 volt 3-wire 3-phase service from a 4160 volt supply line, these transformers should be connected in

   A. delta-wye
   C. delta-delta
   B. wye-wye
   D. wye-delta

   1.____

2. Assume that the full rating of a certain transformer is 190 kw at *95%* power factor. The kva rating of this transformer is MOST NEARLY

   A. 95   B. 200   C. 180   D. 220

   2.____

3. Assume that a load totaling 500 kw is to be supplied. Two 500 kw generators and one 250 kw generator are available.
   Of the following combinations, the MOST efficient operation would be achieved by operating

   A. one 500 kw machine at full load
   B. both 500 kw machines at half load
   C. both 500 dw machines at 200 kw load and the 250 kw machine at 100 kw load
   D. one 500 kw machine at half load and the 250 kw machine at full load

   3.____

4. Assume that the power in a balanced three-wire, three-phase load is measured by the two wattmeter method and is read by means of two wattmeters, W_1 and W2.
   If W_1/W_2 is positive, decreases to zero and then becomes negative, the power factor has changed from

   A. lagging to leading
   B. leading to lagging
   C. a value below .5 to a value above .5
   D. a value above .5 to a value below .5

   4.____

5. Assume that it is required to measure the power in an unbalanced varying three-phase, four-wire, 120/208 volt circuit directly.
   Of the following sets of instruments, the one indicating the minimum number required for this is

   A. an ammeter and a voltmeter
   B. two wattmeters
   C. three wattmeters
   D. four wattmeters

   5.____

19

6. Assume that a certain standard cartridge fuse is loose in its clips.   6.____
   This will result in the

   A. fuse blowing as soon as the full power is turned on
   B. clips becoming hot
   C. fuse blowing out when half of the normal voltage is used
   D. creation of a ground on the circuit

7. Assume that only one of the following instruments is available to measure a certain insu-   7.____
   lation resistance. Of these, the BEST choice is _____ resistance.

   A. ammeter of high   B. voltmeter of low
   C. ammeter of low   D. voltmeter of high

8. If the speed of the prime mover driving the alternator supplying a synchronous motor   8.____
   becomes unstable, the motor will

   A. job   B. plug
   C. overcompound   D. hunt

9. The type of meter used to indicate the phase relation between the voltage and the cur-   9.____
   rent of an AC circuit is called a

   A. phase meter   B. phase difference meter
   C. power factor meter   D. a synchroscope

10. Assume that a circuit breaker equipped with a bellows-type plunger time delay relay   10.____
    opens instantaneously an overload although set for a certain time delay during the last
    inspection.
    The MOST likely cause is

    A. contacts pitted
    B. air vent completely closed
    C. air vent wide open
    D. disk rubbing

11. Assume that there is unequal heating in a bank of transformers connected wye primary   11.____
    and delta secondary.
    Of the following troubles, the one which can cause these symptoms is

    A. overload
    B. ground on one of the primary phases
    C. not sufficient oil in tank
    D. oil saponified on outside of cooling coils

12. Assume that a 3-phase 3-wire 4160 volt system has a balanced three-phase load con-   12.____
    nected to it and that the kva of the load is to be measured by means of an ammeter and
    voltmeter connected through instrument transformers. The CT is rated 200/5 amperes
    and the PT is rated 4160/120. If the voltmeter reads 100 volts and the ammeter reads 4.8
    amperes, the load, in kva, is MOST NEARLY

    A. 1152   B. 33.5   C. 670   D. 8.4

13. Of the following, the one which is an accurate and convenient method of measuring liquid velocity is a   13.____

    A. pitotmeter   B. dynamometer
    C. liquidometer   D. piezometer

14. In a venturi meter, the liquid flows from a large section into a narrow throat. In such a meter, the flow of liquid from the large section to the throat is _____ its static pressure _____ .   14.____

    A. accelerated and; is increased
    B. accelerated and; is reduced
    C. decreased and; is increased
    D. accelerated but; remains the same

15. Of the following statements concerning the oiling of ring-oiled bearings on electric motors, the one which describes the BEST procedure is that ring-oiled bearings should be filled through the   15.____

    A. filler gauge on the side of the bearing housing when the machine is shut down
    B. top when the machine is shut down
    C. top when the machine is running
    D. filler gauge when the machine is running

16. Assume that a vacuum gauge reads 24" of mercury. This is equivalent to an absolute pressure of MOST NEARLY _____ p.s.i.   16.____

    A. 11.8   B. 6.0   C. 8.7   D. 2.9

17. Of the following, the one which BEST describes the function of a prony brake is   17.____

    A. prevent series motors from *running away*
    B. bring prime movers to a very rapid stop
    C. measure the power output of motors
    D. regenerative braking of DC motors

18. Assume that a spur gear having 60 teeth revolves at 720 r.p.m. that drives another spur gear having 80 teeth. The speed, in r.p.m., at which the gear having 80 teeth revolves will be   18.____

    A. 270   B. 540   C. 480   D. 960

19. In an ordering description for a 6" gate valve, it is specified that the valve shall be: I.B.B.M.; O.S.&Y.; and F.E.
Of the following, the one that MOST NEARLY defines these abbreviations is iron   19.____

    A. and brass body mounted, open stem and yoke, flanged end
    B. body brass mounted, open stem and yoke, fluted end
    C. body brass mounted, open stem and yoke, flanged end
    D. body brass mounted, open seat and yoke, flanged end

20. The surge caused by sudden opening or closing of valves in a closed liquid piping system is USUALLY called   20.____

    A. jetting   B. precipitation
    C. water hammer   D. tailing

21. Of the following, the MOST likely location for an *after-cooler* on a super-charged dual fuel diesel engine is

    A. between the turbocharger and the intake manifold
    B. in the fuel injection system
    C. between the lubricating oil filter and the sump tank
    D. in the day tank

21.____

22. Dual-fuel diesel engines USUALLY require

    A. afterburners
    B. carburetors
    C. spark plugs to initiate ignition
    D. pilot injection of liquid fuel to initiate ignition

22.____

23. Assume that an engine has a no-load speed of 370 r.p.m. and a full load speed of 360 r.p.m.
The speed regulation of this engine is MOST NEARLY

    A. .98%   B. 2.2%   C. 1.1%   D. 2.75%

23.____

24. Assume that a given centrifugal pump requires 100 h.p. when operating at 1000 r.p.m. A required increase in the capacity and the head makes it necessary to operate at 1100 r.p.m.
Under these conditions, the required power is MOST NEARLY _____ HP.

    A. 101   B. 123   C. 110   D. 133

24.____

25. Assume that 60,000 gpm of water at 60F are to be raised through a lift of 33 feet.
If the efficiency of the pump is 50% and a gallon of water weighs 8.3 pounds, then the horsepower required to drive the pump is MOST NEARLY

    A. 600   B. 1000   C. 800   D. 1200

25.____

26. Assume that a certain pumping station has three pumps A, B, and C. A can pump 1000 gallons in 6 minutes, B can pump 1000 gallons in 3 minutes, and C can pump 1000 gallons in 2 minutes.
The time required for all three pumps, working at the same time, to pump 1000 gallons is MOST NEARLY _____ minute(s).

    A. 2   B. 1   C. 1 1/2   D. 1/2

26.____

27. Assume that a centrifugal pump that is used to pump water has a water seal ring in its stuffing box.
Of the following, the MAIN purpose of the water seal ring in such a case is to prevent

    A. water from leaking out of the pump into the stuffing box
    B. water from getting into the packing
    C. air from entering the pump through the packing box
    D. water from leaking out of the stuffing box

27.____

28. For a given centrifugal pump, the quantity of water delivered will vary _____ the speed.

    A. directly as
    B. inversely as

28.____

C. directly as the square of
D. inversely as the square of

29. Assume that two identical centrifugal pumps are operated in series.   29.____
Under these conditions, the _____ at which they operate together at a given _____ .

    A. capacity; head is a quarter of that for a single pump
    B. head; capacity is double that for a single pump
    C. efficiency; capacity is half that for a single pump
    D. capacity; head is double that for a given pump

30. For a given centrifugal pump, the head will vary   30.____

    A. directly as the square root of the speed
    B. directly as the speed
    C. inversely as the speed
    D. directly as the square of the speed

31. Of the following, the MAIN purpose of the volute casing on a centrifugal pump is to   31.____

    A. convert its velocity head into pressure
    B. provide a chamber for priming the pump
    C. aid in venting the pump
    D. convert its pressure head to velocity

32. Of the following types of pumps, the one NOT generally used as a diesel fuel transfer   32.____
pump is the _____ type.

    A. gear   B. screw
    C. lobe   D. reciprocating

33. Of the following oils, the one which is the HEAVIEST is S.A.E.   33.____

    A. 10   B. 30   C. 20   D. 40

34. Of the following, a well-planned safety program should NOT be expected to   34.____

    A. help develop safe work habits and attitudes
    B. focus attention on specific accident causes
    C. compensate for unsafe conditions and procedures
    D. improve employee and management relations

35. Of the following, the one which describes the safest method for using an adjustable   35.____
wrench is with the open jaw facing _____ on the handle.

    A. the user, pull
    B. the user, push
    C. away from the user, pull
    D. away from the user, push

36. Of the following basic techniques for preventing accidental injury, the one which is MOST   36.____
effective is

    A. make the workers aware of the hazard and train them to avoid it
    B. control the hazard by guarding it

C. eliminate the hazard from the plant
D. encourage the use of protective devices to shield the men against the hazard

37. Portable electric power tools permanently marked with the words *double insulated* and which have been so listed by the Underwriters' Laboratories, Inc. can be safely used 37.____

    A. without third wire grounding
    B. only with polarized receptacles
    C. to work on *live* equipment
    D. in areas containing high concentrations of volatilized flammable solvents

38. When using a two-section extension ladder with an extended length of 60 feet, the one of the following which is NOT a safe action is 38.____

    A. face the ladder when ascending
    B. face the ladder when descending
    C. allow a maximum of 2 feet of overlap
    D. place the foot about 15 feet from the wall

39. Of the following, the type of fire extinguisher which is NEVER suitable for use on an elec- trical fire is 39.____

    A. liquefied gas   B. dry chemical
    C. carbon dioxide   D. gas cartridge actuated

40. Assume that a member of your crew has been seriously injured by an accident in the plant.
Of the following, the FIRST thing that should be done is 40.____

    A. determine the cause of the accident
    B. order the rest of the crew back to work
    C. notify your supervisor
    D. assist the injured man

KEY (CORRECT ANSWERS)

1.	D	11.	B, C	21.	A	31.	A
2.	B	12.	A	22.	D	32.	D
3.	A	13.	A	23.	D	33.	D
4.	D	14.	B	24.	D	34.	C
5.	C	15.	A, B	25.	B	35.	A
6.	B	16.	D	26.	B	36.	C
7.	D	17.	C	27.	C	37.	A
8.	D	18.	B	28.	A	38.	C
9.	C	19.	C	29.	B	39.	A, D
10.	C	20.	C	30.	D	40.	D

EXAMINATION SECTION
TEST 1

DIRECTIONS: Each question or incomplete statement is followed by several suggested answers or completions. Select the one that BEST answers the question or completes the statement. *PRINT THE LETTER OF THE CORRECT ANSWER IN THE SPACE AT THE RIGHT.*

1. The direction of rotation of a d.c. shunt motor can be reversed by reversing   1.____

    A. the line leads
    B. both the armature and field current
    C. the field or armature current
    D. the current in one pole winding

2. The insulation resistance of the stator winding of an induction motor is MOST commonly measured or tested with a(n)   2.____

    A. strobe   B. ammeter   C. megger   D. S-meter

3. Assume that three 12-ohm resistances are connected in delta across a 208-volt, 3-phase circuit. The line current, in amperes, will be MOST NEARLY   3.____

    A. 30   B. 20.4   C. 17.32   D. 8.66

4. Assume that three 12 ohm resistances are connected in wye across a 208-volt, 3-phase circuit. The power, in watts, dissipated in this resistance load will be MOST NEARLY   4.____

    A. 4200   B. 3600   C. 1200   D. 900

5. The one of the following knots which is MOST commonly used to shorten a rope without cutting it is the   5.____

    A. clove hitch   B. diamond knot
    C. sheepshank   D. square knot

6. Assume that it is required to pump 40 M.G.D. of water against a 65 ft. head. If the pump efficiency is 65%, the B.H.P. of this pump is MOST NEARLY   6.____

    A. 920   B. 700   C. 460   D. 176

7. Assume that a pump had to be shut down temporarily due to trouble which was first reported by an oiler. The one of the following entries in the log concerning this occurrence which is LEAST important is the   7.____

    A. time of the shutdown
    B. period of time the pump was out of service
    C. cause of the trouble
    D. time the oiler came on shift

8. At sea level, the theoretical maximum distance, in feet, that water can be lifted by suction only is MOST NEARLY   8.____

    A. 12.00   B. 14.70   C. 33.57   D. 72.0

9. While a lubricating oil is in use, for good performance, its neutralization number should   9.____

    A. keep rising
    B. remain about the same
    C. be greater than 0.1
    D. be greater than 2.0

10. Cast iron castings that need repairing are USUALLY repaired by the process known as   10.____

    A. electric arc welding
    B. electro-forming
    C. brazing
    D. resistance welding

11. The term SAE stands for   11.____

    A. Standard Auto Engines
    B. Standard Air Engines
    C. Society of Automotive Engineers
    D. Society of Aviation Engineers

12. The parts of a large sewage pump that would MOST likely need repairs after the least number of hours of operation are the   12.____

    A. pump casings
    B. impellers
    C. wearing rings
    D. outboard bearings

13. Assume that the power in a balanced three-phase load is measured by the two wattmeter method and is read by means of two wattmeters, namely W_1 and W_2. If the power factor of the load is .5 leading,   13.____

    A. W_1 will read positive and W_2 will read negative
    B. W_1 will read negative and W_2 will read positive
    C. both W_1 and W_2 will read negative
    D. W_1 will read positive and W_2 will read zero

14. The current in amperes of a 220-volt 5-H.P., d.c. motor having an efficiency of 90% is MOST NEARLY   14.____

    A. 18.8   B. 17   C. 14.3   D. 20.5

15. A shunt generator having an armature current of 50 amperes, an armature resistance of .05 ohms, and a generated e.m.f. of 222.5 volts will MOST likely have a terminal voltage of _____ volts.   15.____

    A. 172.5   B. 220.0   C. 222.5   D. 225

16. Assume that a 4-pole, 220-volt d.c. motor has a back e.m.f. of 215 volts and 4 armature paths between terminals. If the field flux per pole is suddenly decreased to one-half of its former value, the motor speed, in r.p.m., compared to its original speed will be MOST likely   16.____

    A. decreased to about one-quarter
    B. decreased to about one-half
    C. doubled
    D. increased by one-quarter

17. The frequency of the voltage generated in a synchronous machine having 8 poles and   17.____
    running at 720 r.p.m. is MOST NEARLY

    A. 120   B. 72   C. 60   D. 48

18. Assume that a synchronous converter has two slip rings and a direct current voltage of   18.____
    313 volts between the brushes. The effective alternating voltage between slip rings is
    MOST NEARLY _____ volts.

    A. 220   B. 278   C. 330   D. 440

19. A newly appointed plant engineer attempted to make an emergency repair on a d.c.   19.____
    motor which had an open armature coil (lap wound) by completely cutting this coil in two
    and disconnecting it from both commutator bars and then running an insulated jumper
    large enough to safely carry the current between the two bars. This attempted emer-
    gency repair will

    A. result in an inoperative motor
    B. not significantly affect the normal running of the motor
    C. cause the motor to emit vicious purplish sparks at the commutator while running
    D. cause the motor to overheat excessively while running

20. The purpose of full wave rectifiers is to   20.____

    A. produce a.c. current which contains some d.c.
    B. change d.c. current to a.c.
    C. produce d.c. current having an a.c. ripple of twice the input frequency
    D. produce only a.c. current having twice the input frequency

21. The temporary production of a substitute for a two-phase current so as to obtain a make-   21.____
    shift rotating field in starting a single phase motor is called

    A. phase splitting   B. pole pitch
    C. phase transformation   D. pole splitting

22. In a fully charged lead acid storage battery, the active material in the positive plates is   22.____

    A. sponge lead   B. lead carbonate
    C. lead acetate   D. lead peroxide

23. A heat exchanger commonly located between the low pressure and high pressure cylin-   23.____
    ders of an air compressor is used to _____ of the compressor air.

    A. lower the temperature
    B. increase the relative humidity
    C. decrease the relative humidity
    D. raise the temperature

24. The one of the following instruments which is used for the determination of the velocity of   24.____
    air in ducts is the

    A. psychrometer   B. pitot tube
    C. U gage   D. spherometer

25. A high tension breaker (4160 volts) should be equipped with a mechanical interlock which will prevent the breaker from being raised or advanced into, and lowered or withdrawn from, the operating position unless   25.____

 A. it is open
 B. it is closed
 C. the full load is connected
 D. a light load is connected

26. For the operation of a high tension breaker (4160 volts), the suitable control voltage for BEST performance is usually   26.____

 A. 600 volts a.c.   B. 600 volts d.c.
 C. 208 to 440 volts a.c.   D. 70 to 140 volts d.c.

27. The equipment on which you would be MOST likely to find an unloader is a(n)   27.____

 A. centrifugal water pump   B. air compressor
 C. vacuum pump   D. steam engine

28. The term Saybolt refers to a measure of   28.____

 A. specific gravity   B. boiling point
 C. hardness   D. viscosity

29. Assume that a centrifugal fan running at 750 r.p.m. delivers 20,000 c.f.m. at a static pressure of one inch. If this fan is required to deliver 28,000 c.f.m., at the same static pressure, it should be run at a speed, in r.p.m., of MOST NEARLY   29.____

 A. 1500   B. 1250   C. 1150   D. 1050

30. The horsepower of a fan varies as the _____ of the fan speed.   30.____

 A. cube   B. square
 C. square root   D. cube root

31. The gearing for transmitting power between two shafts at right angles to each other consists of two essential parts: 31.____

 A. two worm wheels   B. a worm and bevel gear
 C. a rack and pinion   D. two bevel gears

32. If a transmission main drive gear, having 30 teeth, rotates at 400 r.p.m. and drives a counter shaft gear at 300 r.p.m., the total number of teeth on the countershaft drive will be   32.____

 A. 30   B. 40   C. 60   D. 80

33. The one of the following faults of a C.B. main contact which is NOT a cause of overheating of air circuit breakers is   33.____

 A. excessive pressure
 B. insufficient area in contact
 C. oxidized contacts
 D. dirty contacts

34. The MAIN reason that larger size electrical cables (such as #0000) are always stranded   34.____
    rather than solid is that they

    A. are more flexible
    B. are stronger
    C. have a higher conductivity
    D. have a higher specific resistance

Questions 35-37.

DIRECTIONS: Questions 35 through 37, inclusive, are to be answered in accordance with the
                diagram of the auto transformer and data below.

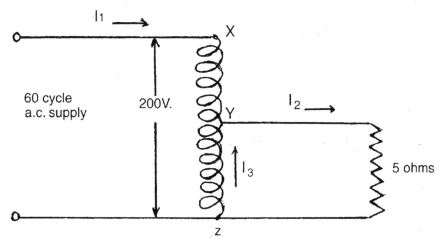

Data: An auto transformer whose primary is XZ is connected across a 200-volt a.c. supply as shown in the above diagram. The load of 5 ohms is connected across Y and Z.
(Assume that point Y is the mid-point of the winding.)

35. The current I_1, in amperes, is APPROXIMATELY equal to   35.____

    A. 5   B. 10   C. 15   D. 20

36. The current I_2, in amperes, is APPROXIMATELY equal to   36.____

    A. 5   B. 10   C. 15   D. 20

37. The current I_3, in amperes, is APPROXIMATELY equal to   37.____

    A. 5   B. 10   C. 15   D. 20

38. Assume that you see one of your oilers tumble down a long flight of concrete steps and   38.____
    fall heavily on the lower landing. You rush to him and find that he is unconscious but
    breathing. Of the following, the BEST course of action for you to take is

    A. have two of your men carry him to the office and summon a doctor
    B. do not move him but cover him with a blanket and call a doctor
    C. prop him upright and let him inhale spirits of ammonia and call a doctor
    D. prepare a bed of blankets and have two of your men lift him on it, then summon a
       doctor

39. It is sometimes desirable to have a control that will cause a d.c. motor to come to a standstill quickly instead of coasting to a standstill after the stop button is pressed. This result is MOST commonly obtained by means of an action called

    A. counter e.m.f. method   B. armature reaction
    C. diverting   D. dynamic braking

39.____

40. In an electric circuit, a high-spot-temperature is MOST commonly due to

    A. an open circuit
    B. a defective connection
    C. intermittent use of circuit
    D. excessive distribution voltage

40.____

———

KEY (CORRECT ANSWERS)

1.	C	11.	C	21.	A	31.	D
2.	C	12.	C	22.	D	32.	B
3.	A	13.	D	23.	A	33.	A
4.	B	14.	A	24.	B	34.	A
5.	C	15.	B	25.	A	35.	B
6.	B	16.	C	26.	D	36.	D
7.	D	17.	D	27.	B	37.	B
8.	C	18.	A	28.	D	38.	B
9.	B	19.	B	29.	D	39.	D
10.	C	20.	C	30.	A	40.	B

———

TEST 2

DIRECTIONS: Each question or incomplete statement is followed by several suggested answers or completions. Select the one that BEST answers the question or completes the statement. *PRINT THE LETTER OF THE CORRECT ANSWER IN THE SPACE AT THE RIGHT.*

1. The MAIN reason for periodic inspections and testing of equipment in an electrically powered plant is to   1.____

    A.   keep the men busy at all times
    B.   familiarize the men with the equipment
    C.   train the men to be ready in an emergency
    D.   discover minor faults before they have a chance to become significantly serious

2. Assume that an employee calls up to give advance notice of his intentions to be absent the following day. The MOST important information that he should give is   2.____

    A.   the exact time of calling
    B.   the balance of his sick leave time
    C.   the reason for his absence
    D.   name of attending doctor

3. The MAIN reason why a plant mechanic who is assigned to service equipment must be able to make proper adjustments and repairs quickly is that   3.____

    A.   equipment always deteriorates rapidly unless readjusted immediately
    B.   idle equipment will result in poor plant efficiency and work delays
    C.   the ability to work rapidly is the result of extensive training and experience
    D.   he will have more time for his other duties

4. A 1300-volt, three-phase system with a grounded neutral has a phase to ground voltage of APPROXIMATELY   4.____

    A.   440   B.   600   C.   690   D.   750

5. A 220-volt, 40-H.P. induction motor is given an insulation resistance test. The normal value of the insulating resistance, in megohms, for this motor is MOST NEARLY   5.____

    A.   0.2   B.   0.4   C.   0.05   D.   0.95

6. To increase the range of an a.c. ammeter, the one of the following which is MOST commonly used is a(n)   6.____

    A.   current transformer   B.   inductance
    C.   condenser   D.   straight copper bar

7. When batteries are being charged, they should not be exposed to open flames and sparks because of the flammability of   7.____

    A.   hydrogen   B.   oxygen
    C.   sulphurous gas   D.   fuming sulphuric acid

8. Assume that you and your supervisor are on an inspectional tour of the outdoor equipment of the plant and that a co-worker suddenly falls unconscious on the pavement. If on close observation you find that the victim is not breathing, the FIRST of the following things to do is

    A. move the victim indoors
    B. notify his family
    C. administer first aid to restore breathing
    D. nothing, but summon a doctor

8.____

9. Assume that one of your men, who has always been efficient, industrious, and conscientious, suddenly becomes lax in his work, makes numerous mistakes, and shuns responsibilities. The cause of such a change

    A. is usually that the man is responding to a minor change in the job situation
    B. is usually apparent to the stationary engineer in charge and fellow workers
    C. may be quickly found by a close study of reports and personnel records
    D. may have no direct relationship to any change in the job situation

9.____

Questions 10-12.

DIRECTIONS: Questions 10 through 12, inclusive, are to be answered in accordance with the diagram of a 3-phase transformer and data given below.

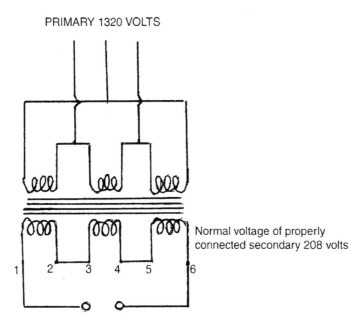

PRIMARY 1320 VOLTS

Normal voltage of properly connected secondary 208 volts

Data: The above transformer is to be connected delta-delta, with primary connections completed as shown. Assume that the connections of the secondary of the transformer bank are not completed and it is found that coil (1-2) is reversed. Under this condition:

10. The voltage between points 6 and 3 will be MOST NEARLY

    A. 208   B. 360   C. 416   D. 520

10.____

11. The voltage between points 1 and 6 will be MOST NEARLY   11._____

    A. 208   B. 360   C. 416   D. 520

12. The voltage between points 1 and 4 will be MOST NEARLY   12._____

    A. 208   B. 360   C. 416   D. 520

13. The one of the following types of valves which is GENERALLY used where extremely   13._____
    close regulation of flow is needed is the _____ valve.

    A. gate   B. glove   C. needle   D. blow-off

14. Lubricating oils of mineral origin are refined from _____ products.   14._____

    A. lard-beef   B. cotton seed
    C. crude petroleum   D. lime soap

Questions 15-17.

DIRECTIONS: Questions 15 through 17, inclusive, are to be answered in accordance with the
                      diagram below.

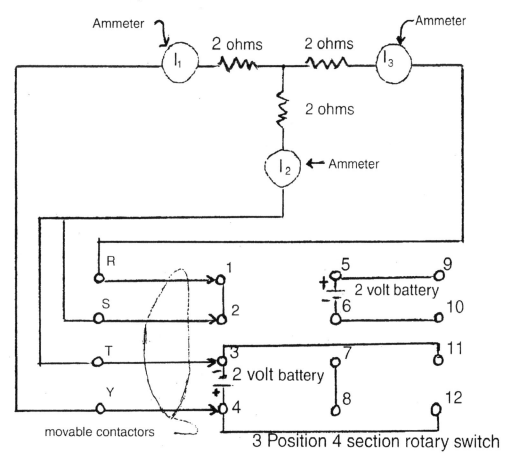

3 Position 4 section rotary switch

15. When switch movable contactors R, S, T, and V are in position 1, 2, 3, and 4, as shown,   15._____
    the current I_1, in amperes, is MOST NEARLY

    A. 2   B. 2/3   C. 1/3   D. 1/6

16. When switch movable contactors R, S, T, and V are in position 5, 6, 7, and 8, the current   16.____
    I_2, in amperes, is MOST NEARLY

    A. 2   B. 2/3   C. 1/3   D. 1/6

17. When switch movable contactors R, S, T, and V are in position 9, 10, 11, and 12, the cur-   17.____
    rent, in amperes, registered by ammeter I_3 is MOST NEARLY

    A. 3   B. 2   C. 2/3   D. 1/3

18. Light-bodied lubricating oils are MOST commonly used for   18.____
    A. light loads at high speeds
    B. heavy bearing pressure
    C. heavy loads at slow speeds
    D. chain drives and gears

19. The one of the following lubricants which is LEAST likely to be attacked by acids is   19.____
    A. cottonseed oil   B. castor oil
    C. rape seed oil   D. graphite

20. In general, non-rising stem gate valves are BEST adaptable for   20.____
    A. use where frequent adjustments are necessary
    B. installations carrying viscous liquids
    C. throttling or close control
    D. places where space is a factor

21. The presence of moisture in insulating oil is undesirable. The percentage of moisture   21.____
    which will reduce the dielectric strength of insulating oil to approximately one-half of its
    dielectric strength when dry is MOST NEARLY _____ of moisture.

    A. 0.5%   B. 0.05%   C. 0.005%   D. 0.0005%

22. It has been brought to your attention that one of the men under your supervision is com-   22.____
    plaining to fellow co-workers that another man has received an easy assignment through
    his *connections*. In this situation, it is BEST to

    A. privately inform the man who is complaining of the truth regarding the assignment
    B. in the presence of others, demand absolute proof from the man who is complaining
    C. ignore the matter since it is not your job to interfere in disagreements between the
       men
    D. tell the complaining man to apply for a desirable assignment also

23. In the standard method of testing electrical insulating oils, the test cup used to determine   23.____
    the dielectric strength contains two electrodes, each _____ inch in diameter with a gap
    of _____ inch between them.

    A. 0.1; 1   B. 0.5; 0.3   C. 0.75; 0.3   D. 1.00; 0.1

24. The PROPER fire extinguishing agent to use to extinguish fires in electrical equipment is   24.____
    A. water   B. foam
    C. soda-acid   D. carbon dioxide

25. Circuit conductors operating at 600 volts or less may be worked upon live, without open-   25.____
ing the circuit, if certain precautionary measures are taken. The one of the following that
BEST represents one of these precautionary measures for this work is

    A. bare or exposed places on one conductor must be taped after another conductor is
first exposed
    B. adjacent live or grounded conductor shall be covered with a conducting material
    C. bare or exposed places on one conductor must be taped before another conductor
is exposed
    D. adjacent live or grounded conductors shall be securely bonded to ground

26. In order to properly distribute the load (in proportion to their rated capacities) between   26.____
two alternators which are operating in parallel, it is necessary to

    A. overexcite the smaller alternator and underexcite the larger one
    B. adjust the governor on the prime mover
    C. underexcite the larger alternator but use normal excitation on the smaller one
    D. underexcite the smaller alternator and overexcite the larger one

27. If a large amount of flame is visible from a small pile of burning material, it is likely that   27.____
the material MUST contain a substance that

    A. contains a large amount of inorganic material
    B. produces during the burning process a large amount of pure carbon
    C. produces during the burning process a large amount of combustible gases or
vapors
    D. is composed almost entirely of pure carbon

28. If the velocity of water flow in a pipe is doubled, assuming other factors are constant, the   28.____
loss of head due to friction will be

    A. decreased 1/2 times   B. decreased 1/4 times
    C. increased 4 times   D. the same

29. Reprimanding a subordinate for inefficiency in the presence of fellow co-workers is apt to   29.____

    A. cause the subordinate to resign
    B. arouse the subordinate's resentment
    C. improve the performance of all present
    D. cause the subordinate to improve

30. Assume that certain work assignments are not liked by any of your subordinates.   30.____
Because this work has to be done, you, as the operator in charge, should try as much as
possible to

    A. assign this work as punishment details
    B. rotate the work assignments among subordinates
    C. assign this work to the best-natured man
    D. assign this work to the junior men

31. A senior engineer, in discussing new departmental regulations with his subordinates,   31.____
commented, *We should be conscious of the fact that our interests are mutual, and that
by all of us in unison putting our shoulder to the wheel and working together, we can
achieve our common objective.* This approach is

A. *good,* because this attitude will promote cooperation
B. *poor,* because this approach will invite excessive criticism
C. *good,* because it will promote good fellowship
D. *poor,* because this will invite too much familiarity

32. In the inspection of relays, the type of trouble generally encountered often depends on the type of relay. The one of the following which is NOT a trouble encountered with an induction-type relay is

    32.____

A. friction between disc and magnet
B. dust on disc
C. foreign matter in the gear train
D. punctured bellows

33. With reference to diesel engines, the one of the following which is NOT a method of scavenging the cylinder is _____ scavenging.

    33.____

A. crankcase
B. integral
C. under-piston
D. vane

34. Direct current motors for BEST performance should have their brushes set on the commutator

    34.____

A. at the neutral point (under load)
B. at the point of maximum armature reaction
C. radially at an angle of 90 (leading)
D. radially at an angle of 80 (leading)

35. The PROPER order of events that take place in a 4-stroke cycle diesel engine is _____, and exhaust.

    35.____

A. air intake, power expansion, compression
B. air intake, compression, power expansion
C. power expansion, air intake, compression
D. compression, air intake, power expansion

36. The compression ratio of a diesel engine that has no starting ignition device is GENERALLY in the range of

    36.____

A. 11 to 20
B. 8 to 10
C. 6 to 8
D. 4 to 6

37. The base in a lubricating grease denotes the

    37.____

A. type of soap that is used in its manufacture
B. consistency and the texture of the grease
C. dropping or melting point of the grease
D. carbon-residue content of the grease

38. Of the following sets of pipes, the one having a total combined area exactly equal to the area of a 12" diameter pipe is _____ pipes.

    38.____

A. two 6"
B. two 8"
C. one 8" pipe and two 6"
D. four 6"

39. Assume that a single phase load takes EI x .8 watts, where E is the line voltage, I the line current, and .8 the power factor. The rating in volt-amperes of the synchronous condenser needed to raise the power factor to unity is MOST NEARLY EI x   39.____

   A. .6   B. .8   C. .9   D. 1

40. If rubber gloves commonly used on high tension work are found on test to have pinholes, they   40.____

   A. may be used on low voltage
   B. should be discarded
   C. should be patched with rubber tape
   D. may be used only in dry places

KEY (CORRECT ANSWERS)

1.	D	11.	C	21.	C	31.	A
2.	C	12.	B	22.	A	32.	D
3.	B	13.	C	23.	D	33.	D
4.	D	14.	C	24.	D	34.	A
5.	A	15.	B	25.	C	35.	B
6.	A	16.	C	26.	B	36.	A
7.	A	17.	D	27.	C	37.	A
8.	C	18.	A	28.	C	38.	D
9.	D	19.	D	29.	B	39.	A
10.	A	20.	D	30.	B	40.	B

EXAMINATION SECTION
TEST 1

DIRECTIONS: Each question or incomplete statement is followed by several suggested answers or completions. Select the one that BEST answers the question or completes the statement. *PRINT THE LETTER OF THE CORRECT ANSWER IN THE SPACE AT THE RIGHT.*

1. Assume that an engine has a no-load speed of 1800 RPM and a full-load speed of 1650 RPM,
   The speed regulation of this engine is MOST NEARLY   1____

   A. 12%.   B. 11%   C. 9.1%   D. 8.4%

2. The color of the third wire used for grounding portable electric power tools is generally   2____

   A. black   B. white   C. red   D. green

3. A series circuit consists of a pure inductance and a pure resistance. When an AC voltage is impressed across such a circuit, the _____ the resistence by 90 degrees.   3____

   A. current in the inductance lags the current in
   B. current in the inductance leads the current in
   C. voltage across the inductance lags the voltage across
   D. voltage across the inductance leads the voltage across

4. Of the following devices, the one which should be used for throttling of water going through it is the _____ valve.   4____

   A. gate   B. globe   C. check   D. relief

5. If the line-to-line voltage of a wye-connected 3-phase system is 220 volts AC and the phase current is 10 amperes, then the total power delivered is MOST NEARLY _____ watts.   5____

   A. 1270   B. 2200   C. 3800   D. 6600

6. The sensitivity of a meter movement is given as 50 microamperes. This is equivalent to a voltmeter rating of _____ ohms/volt.   6____

   A. 50,000   B. 20,000   C. 50   D. 20

7. Doubling the number of turns of an inductor should _____ its original value.   7____

   A. *reduce* the inductance to one-quarter of
   B. *reduce* the inductance to one-half of
   C. *increase* the inductance to twice
   D. *increase* the inductance to four times

8. Electrical fuses are rated in   8____

   A. current and voltage   B. current and wattage
   C. ampere-hours   D. watt-hours

9. A 30-ohm resistor is placed in parallel with an inductor that has an inductive reactance of 40 ohms. If 120 volts AC is impressed across the parallel combination, the *total current* drawn from the 120-volt AC line is _____ amps.

    A. 1.7   B. 2.4   C. 3.0   D. 5.0

9____

10. The symbol shown at the right, found in the schematic of a motor control circuit represents a

    A. silicon-controlled rectifier
    B. thyratron
    C. heat-sunk diode
    D. thermal overload

10____

11. A device that can be used to check the condition of the electrolyte in a storage battery is the

    A. hygrometer   B. hydrometer
    C. hydrostat   D. aquastat

11____

12. Of the following, the BEST device to use to check the condition of the insulation of a cable is the

    A. ohmmeter   B. wheatstone bridge
    C. voltmeter   D. megger

12____

13. The decibel is a unit used in measuring the level of

    A. magnetization   B. acidity
    C. sound   D. contamination

13____

14. A rectangular bus bar with a cross-section of.1.0 inch x .50 inch has a cross-sectional area MOST NEARLY equivalent to _____ circular mils.

    A. 250,000   B. 640,000
    C. 1,000,000   D. 1,280,000

14____

15. The electrical conductivity of copper is lower than that of

    A. silver   B. gold   C. carbon   D. aluminum

15____

16. A voltmeter has a ground connection and two terminals, one of which is used for 0-300 volts and the other for 0-750 volts. The scale is marked only for the 0-750 range.
A scale reading of 200, when the 0-300 volt range is being used, corresponds to an actual voltage of _____ volts.

    A. 200   B. 160   C. 120   D. 80

16____

17. When putting out a fire with a hand extinguisher, it is BEST to direct the discharge at the _____ the fire.

    A. base of   B. area behind
    C. area in front of   D. highest flames of

17____

40

18. Someone suggests that the silver-plated main contacts of a circuit breaker be cleaned with fine sandpaper. This suggestion is

18____

    A. *poor,* since the useful silver plating would be removed
    B. *good,* since you would be removing silver oxide which is a poor conductor
    C. *good,* since this will prevent overheating of the circuit breaker
    D. *poor,* since this will change the adjustment of the main contacts

19. If a multi-scale DC voltmeter reads downscale (goes below zero) when connected across two pins of an electrical connector, it is MOST likely that the

19____

    A. meter is defective
    B. voltage across the pins is AC
    C. meter leads are reversed
    D. wrong scale is being used

20. Measurements of illumination in a work area are made with light meters which measure in units of

20____

    A. foot-lamberts   B. foot-candles
    C. lumens   D. watts

21. Assume that new types of circuit breakers and controls are to be installed in the plant where you work. This equipment is to be operated and maintained by you. Of the following, the FIRST step you should take to become familiar with the new equipment is to

21____

    A. read the instruction books for the equipment
    B. call in the manufacturer's field personnel for instructions
    C. read textbooks on the general theory of such equipment
    D. make trial disassemblies and reassemblies of the equipment

22. Of the following, the BEST way to lift a heavy object is to

22____

    A. keep legs spread apart and straight, slowly bending at the waist to grasp the object
    B. place the feet about shoulder-width apart and slowly bend at the knees to reach down to the object
    C. keep legs straight and close together, slowly bending at the waist to grasp the object
    D. place feet close together, and with legs and back straight, bend at the waist to reach down and quickly lift the object

23. Sparks and open flames should be kept away from storage batteries that are being charged because of the high combustibility of the

23____

    A. electrolytes in the batteries
    B. battery cases when hot
    C. gases being produced
    D. sulfuric acid fumes being generated

24. A 16-foot wood ladder is to be leaned against a wall. Of the following, the SAFEST distance at which the base of the ladder should be placed from the base of the wall is _____ feet.

24____

    A. 4   B. 6   C. 8   D. 9

25. Of the following fittings, the one used to connect two lengths of conduit in a straight line is a(n)   25____

    A. elbow   B. nipple   C. tee   D. coupling

26. If a nut is to be tightened to an exact specified value, the wrench that should be used is a(n) _____ wrench.   26____

    A. torque   B. lock-j aw   C. alligator   D. spanner

27. Unloaders are generally found on   27____

    A. centrifugal pumps   B. air compressors
    C. flexible couplings   D. surge suppressors

28. A compound gauge indicates   28____

    A. pressures in lbs. and vacuums in inches of water
    B. both pressures and vacuums in lbs. per sq. inch
    C. pressures in lbs. per sq. inch and vacuums in inches of mercury
    D. pressures in lbs. and vacuums in inches of mercury per sq. inch

29. Of the following, the metal that is used for bearing linings is   29____

    A. Muntz metal   B. duraluminum
    C. naval brass   D. babbitt

30. It has been discovered that the commutator of an electrical machine has developed a flat spot.   30____
To remove the flat spot, the

    A. entire commutator should be ground or turned down until the flat spot is removed
    B. brushes should be changed to a harder grade and the flat spot will eventually wear away
    C. entire commutator should be resurfaced with emery cloth attached to a wooden block which is then pressed against the turning commutator
    D. commutator bars that have the flat spot should be removed for repair or replacement, then reassembled back into the commutator

31. The FIRST operation performed on raw sewage as it comes into a sewage treatment plant is to   31____

    A. add sufficient amounts of chlorine to kill any living organisms
    B. place it into settling tanks to allow sludge to settle to the bottom
    C. pass it through screens to remove or break up coarse material
    D. introduce selected bacteria to initiate biodegrada-tion

32. The MAIN function of diffusers in sewage treatment plants is to   32____

    A. maintain a uniform distribution of non-solubles in the sewage
    B. release compressed air into the sewage
    C. pass the sewage through a fine filter
    D. disperse objectionable and toxic gases that are formed in the sewage

33. A comminutor at a sewage plant is used to   33____

    A. shred sewage matter that is not removed by screens
    B. enable people in one building to talk to people in other buildings
    C. convert AC electric power to DC in the sewage plant
    D. reduce the level of noise in the sewage settling basin building

34. The pH of a substance is an indication of its   34____

    A. resistance to corrosion
    B. magnetic properties
    C. transparency or translucency
    D. acidity or alkalinity

35. Assume that a vacuum gauge reads 15 inches of Hg. The equivalent in *absolute pressure* is MOST NEARLY _____ p.s.i.   35____

    A. 2.0   B. 4.0   C. 7.5   D. 14.7

_____

KEY (CORRECT ANSWERS)

1.	C		16.	D
2.	D		17.	A
3.	D		18.	A
4.	B		19.	C
5.	C		20.	B
6.	B		21.	A
7.	D		22.	B
8.	A		23.	C
9.	D		24.	A
10.	A		25.	D
11.	B		26.	A
12.	D		27.	B
13.	C		28.	C
14.	B		29.	D
15.	A		30.	A

31.	C
32.	B
33.	A
34.	D
35.	C

_____

TEST 2

DIRECTIONS: Each question or incomplete statement is followed by several suggested answers or completions. Select the one that BEST answers the question or completes the statement. *PRINT THE LETTER OF THE CORRECT ANSWER IN THE SPACE AT THE RIGHT.*

1. An ADVANTAGE of a rotary pump over a centrifugal pump is that the rotary pump is   1____

   A. self-priming and requires no valves
   B. better able to handle gritty water
   C. better suited for high pressures and high discharges
   D. quieter and has a pulseless discharge

2. A method used to eliminate water hammer in a water line is to   2____

   A. increase the pressure in the line
   B. use slow-closing valves and faucets
   C. treat the water with a water softener
   D. increase the temperature of the water

3. A pipe nipple that is threaded over its entire length is called a _____ nipple.   3____

   A. shoulder   B. long   C. close   D. short

4. A Stillson wrench is also called a _____ wrench.   4____

   A. strap   B. pipe   C. monkey   D. crescent

5. In a piping diagram, the symbol shown at the right represents a   5____

   A. pressure regulator   B. strainer
   C. check valve   D. drier

6. A shut-off valve is found to have the designation *WOG 300*. The letters WOG mean   6____

   A. Water or Gas Valve
   B. Water, Oil or Gas Pressure
   C. Worthington Gate Valve
   D. Working Gauge Pressure

7. A plunger-type compressed-air-driven reciprocating water pump has a marking *3x4x7*. The number 7 refers to the   7____

   A. diameter of the compressed air piston in inches
   B. diameter of the water piston in inches
   C. length of the stroke in inches
   D. compression ratio

8. Methane is a gas that   8____

   A. has a smell like rotten eggs
   B. is heavier than air
   C. forms the major part of natural gas
   D. is non-combustible

9. As a cylinder in a diesel engine is going through its compression cycle, the air in the cylinder will _____ in pressure and _____ in temperature.   9_____

    A. *decrease; decrease*   B. *increase; increase*
    C. decrease; increase   D. *increase; decrease*

10. A specification for the installation of a storage tank indicates that a hydrostatic test should be made before placing the tank in service.   10_____
A hydrostatic test consists of

    A. immersing the tank, with ports closed, in water and checking for water seeping in
    B. filling the tank with water under pressure and noting how well the pressure is held or whether water leaks out
    C. creating a vacuum in the interior of the tank and noting how well the vacuum is held or whether air leaks in
    D. filling the tank with compressed air and checking for leaks with soapy water

11. When the ignition characteristics of a fuel are represented by a cetane number, the fuel is one that is normally used in a   11_____

    A. gasoline engine   B. gas turbine
    C. diesel engine   D. steam boiler

12. Of the following, a characteristic of a wound-rotor AC induction motor is that it   12_____

    A. provides a wide range of speed control
    B. does not require slip-rings
    C. has a *squirrel cage* armature
    D. operates on single-phase power

13. Detergents are used in lubricating oils to   13_____

    A. reduce the S.A.E. number
    B. prevent oxidation of the oil
    C. keep insoluble matter in suspension
    D. combat corrosion

14. In a four-stroke diesel engine, each piston fires every _____ of the crankshaft.   14_____

    A. one-half revolution   B. revolution
    C. two revolutions   D. four revolutions

15. An electric motor with pressure grease fittings and relief plugs requires lubrication,   15_____
A grease gun should be connected to each fitting and the grease gun should be pumped *until*

    A. grease oozes out along the shaft
    B. grease oozes out from the relief plug hole
    C. the handle becomes hard to move
    D. the handle starts to move freely

16. Of the following, the one which is NOT used for applying grease to a bearing is a(n)   16_____

    A. Alemite fitting   B. grease cup
    C. Zerk fitting   D. pressure plug

17. Of the following, the substance that should be used to melt ice on pavements and walkways is called   17____

    A. calcium chloride   B. trichloroethylene
    C. sodium hydroxide   D. slaked lime

18. On a working drawing, the symbol (shading) given as shown at the right represents   18____

    A. cast iron   B. concrete   C. glass   D. steel

19. A machine screw is indicated on a drawing as The head is the American Standard type called _____ head.   19____

    A. flat   B. oval   C. fillister   D. round

20. The tool that is shown at the right is properly referred to as a(n) _____ tap.   20____

    A. bottoming   B. acme   C. taper   D. plug

21. The tool indicated at the right is referred to as an arch punch.
    This tool should be used to   21____

    A. cut holes in 1/16 inch steel
    B. cut large diameter holes in masonry
    C. run through a conduit prior to pulling a cable or wires
    D. make holes in rubber or leather gasket material

22. Before putting an aerosol container for garbage pickup, it is *good* practice to   22____

    A. puncture it with a screwdriver
    B. use out the contents in normal manner
    C. put it out as is regardless of container contents
    D. remove the spray nozzle

23. A lantern ring is a type of   23____

    A. optical illusion on a light source seen through a fine screen mesh
    B. sealing arrangement used to minimize air leakage between a rotating shaft and a sleeve
    C. piston ring which provides lubrication of the cylinder wall
    D. oil ring bearing lubrication

24. Monel metal is an alloy used for water heater tanks. It is a combination MAINLY of   24____

    A. iron and lead   B. chromium and zinc
    C. nickel and copper   D. vanadium and tin

25. The plumbing fitting shown at the right is called a   25____

   A. Street Elbow
   B. Return Bend
   C. Running Trap
   D. Reversing *El*

26. A galvanized steel plate is a plate with a coating of   26____

   A. lead and tin alloy   B. tin
   C. zinc   D. brass

27. *If* the barrel of a standard micrometer is rotated through one complete revolution, the *gap*   27____
     dimension is changed by _____ inch,

   A. .010   B. .025   C. .100   D. .250

28. Of the following, the indication that a fluorescent lamp is in need of replacement is that   28____

   A. a very low level hum is produced by the ballast
   B. there is a slight delay before the lamp comes up to full brightness after the switch is
       turned on
   C. the lamp flashes on and off, and there are black coatings at the ends
   D. the lamp does not go off each time the switch is turned off

29. The one of the following that is recommended for prime-coating bare metals is   29____

   A. varnish   B. zinc chromate
   C. shellac   D. linseed oil

30. *Dressing* a grinding wheel refers to   30____

   A. replacing the wheel with a new one
   B. reducing the thickness of the wheel
   C. cleaning the grinding surface and making the wheel round
   D. repositioning the wheel on its shaft to eliminate *wobble*

31. A fusible metal plug is a protective device that   31____

   A. melts when the electric current through it exceeds the rating
   B. melts when its temperature reaches a specific figure
   C. ruptures when the pressure behind it goes beyond a certain level
   D. ruptures when the *pull* on it exceeds a specified number of pounds

32. Of the following, the material that is beginning to be used for electrical conduits, plastic   32____
     water pipes, and electrical insulation is

   A. trichloroethyline   B. polyvinylchloride
   C. carbontrichlorofluoride   D. teflon

33. At certain conditions of speed, pressure, and temperature, centrifugal pumps can be made to cavitate.
The conditions causing cavitation

    33____

    A. should be avoided since the impeller may become seriously pitted
    B. result in the highest pump efficiency
    C. produce *water hammer* and should be avoided
    D. also produce the quietest operation of the pump

34. A nut is turned on a 1/2" - 10 bolt.
When the nut is turned through five complete turns on the bolt, the distance it moves longitudinally on the bolt is _____ inch.

    34____

    A. .100   B. .200   C. .375   D. .500

35. A growler is a device used for

    35____

    A. vibrating pipes carrying solid matter
    B. sounding an alarm when hazardous conditions develop
    C. detecting shorts in armatures
    D. chewing up solids in sewage

_____

KEY (CORRECT ANSWERS)

1.	A	16.	D
2.	B	17.	A
3.	C	18.	D
4.	B	19.	B
5.	C	20.	A
6.	B	21.	D
7.	C	22.	B
8.	C	23.	B
9.	B	24.	C
10.	B	25.	B
11.	C	26.	C
12.	A	27.	B
13.	C	28.	C
14.	C	29.	B
15.	B	30.	C

31.	B
32.	B
33.	A
34.	D
35.	C

_____

EXAMINATION SECTION
TEST 1

DIRECTIONS: Each question or incomplete statement is followed by several suggested answers or completions. Select the one that BEST answers the question or completes the statement. *PRINT THE LETTER OF THE CORRECT ANSWER IN THE SPACE AT THE RIGHT.*

1. Assume that certain work assignments are not liked by any of your subordinates. As this work has to be done, you, as the stationary engineer (electric), should try as much as possible to

   A. assign this work as punishment details
   B. rotate the work assignments among subordinates
   C. assign this work to the best-natured man
   D. assign this work to the junior men

   1._____

2. A stationary engineer (electric), in discussing new departmental regulations with his subordinates, commented,
   We should be conscious of the fact that our interests are mutual, and that by all of us in unison putting our shoulders to the wheel and working together, we can achieve our common objective. This approach is _____, because it will _____.

   A. good; promote cooperation
   B. poor; invite excessive criticism
   C. good; promote good fellowship
   D. poor; invite too much familiarity

   2._____

3. In the inspection of relays, the type of trouble encountered often depends on the type of relay.
   The one of the following which is NOT a trouble encountered with an induction-type relay is

   A. friction between disc and magnet
   B. dust on disc
   C. foreign matter in gear train
   D. punctured bellows

   3._____

4. It is sometimes desirable to have a control that will cause a DC motor to come to a standstill quickly instead of coasting to a standstill after the stop button is pressed.
   This result is MOST commonly obtained by means of an action called

   A. counter emf method   B. armature reaction
   C. diverting   D. dynamic braking

   4._____

5. In an electric circuit, a high spot temperature is MOST commonly due to

   A. an open circuit
   B. a defective connection
   C. intermittent use of circuit
   D. excessive distribution voltage

   5._____

6. The MAIN reason for periodic inspections and testing of equipment in an electrically
powered plant is to

   A. keep the men busy at all times
   B. familiarize the men with the equipment
   C. train the men to be ready in an emergency
   D. discover minor faults before they have a chance to become significantly serious

6._____

7. Assume that an employee calls up to give advance notice of his intentions to be absent
the following day.
The MOST important information that he should give is the

   A. exact time of calling
   B. balance of his sick leave time
   C. reason for his absence
   D. name of his attending doctor

7._____

8. The MAIN reason why a stationary engineer who is assigned to service equipment must
be able to make proper adjustments and repairs quickly is that

   A. equipment always deteriorates rapidly unless readjusted immediately
   B. idle equipment will result in poor plant efficiency and work delays
   C. the ability to work rapidly is the result of extensive training and experience
   D. he will have more time for his other duties

8._____

9. Assume that you see one of your oilers tumble down a long flight of concrete steps and
fall heavily on the lower landing. You rush to him and find that he is unconscious but
breathing.
Of the following, the BEST course of action for you to take is

   A. have two of your men carry him into the office and summon a doctor
   B. do not move him but cover him with a blanket and call a doctor
   C. prop him upright and let him inhale spirits of ammonia and call a doctor
   D. prepare a bed of blankets and have two of your men lift him on it; then summon a
      doctor

9._____

10. The MAIN reason that larger size electrical cables (such as #0000) are always stranded
rather than solid is that they

   A. are more flexible
   B. are stronger
   C. have a higher conductivity
   D. have a higher specific resistance

10._____

11. The purpose of full wave rectifiers is to

   A. produce AC current which contains some DC
   B. change DC current to AC
   C. produce DC current having an AC ripple of twice the input frequency
   D. produce only AC current having twice the input frequency

11._____

12. The temporary production of a substitute for a two-phase current so as to obtain a make-   12.____
shift rotating field in starting a single phase motor is called

    A. phase splitting   B. pole pitch
    C. phase transformation   D. pole splitting

13. When batteries are being charged, they should NOT be exposed to open flames and   13.____
sparks because of the flammability of

    A. hydrogen   B. oxygen
    C. sulphurous gas   D. fuming sulphuric acid

14. Assume that you and your supervisor are on an inspectional tour of the outdoor equip-   14.____
ment of the plant and that a co-worker suddenly falls unconscious on the pavement.
If, on close observation, you find that the victim is not breathing, the FIRST thing to do
is

    A. move the victim indoors
    B. notify his family
    C. administer first aid to restore breathing
    D. nothing, but summon a doctor

15. Assume that one of your men, who has always been efficient, industrious, and conscien-   15.____
tious, suddenly becomes lax in his work, makes numerous mistakes, and shuns
responsibilities.
The cause of such a change

    A. is usually that the man is responding to a minor change in the job situation
    B. is usually apparent to the stationary engineer in charge and fellow workers
    C. may be quickly found by a close study of reports and personnel records
    D. may have no direct relationship to any change in the job situation

16. Circuit conductors operating at 600 volts or less may be worked upon live, without open-   16.____
ing the circuit, if certain precautionary measures are taken.
The one of the following that BEST represents one of these precautionary measures
for this work is:

    A. Bare or exposed places on one conductor must be taped after another conductor is
        first exposed
    B. Adjacent live or grounded conductors shall be covered with a conducting material
    C. Bare or exposed places on one conductor must be taped before another conductor
        is exposed
    D. Adjacent live or grounded conductors shall be securely bonded to the ground

17. In order to properly distribute the load (in proportion to their rated capacities) between   17.____
two alternators which are operating in parallel, it is necessary to

    A. overexcite the smaller alternator and underexcite the larger one
    B. adjust the governor on the prime mover
    C. underexcite the larger alternator, but use normal excitation on the smaller one
    D. underexcite the smaller alternator and overexcite the larger one

18. If a large amount of flame is visible from a small pile of burning material, the material must contain a substance that

   18.____

    A. contains a large amount of inorganic material
    B. produces, during the burning process, a large amount of pure carbon
    C. produces, during the burning process, a large amount of combustible gases or vapors
    D. is composed almost entirely of pure carbon

19. In the zeolite process for water treatment, calcium and magnesium are removed by

   19.____

    A. absorption
    C. settling
    B. evaporation
    D. filtration

20. Reprimanding a subordinate for inefficiency in the presence of fellow co-workers is apt to

   20.____

    A. cause the subordinate to resign
    B. arouse the subordinate's resentment
    C. improve the performance of all present
    D. cause the subordinate to improve

21. A heat exchanger commonly located between the low pressure and high pressure cylinders of an air compressor is used to _____ of the compressor air.

   21.____

    A. lower the temperature
    B. increase the relative humidity
    C. decrease the relative humidity
    D. raise the temperature

22. The one of the following instruments which is used for the determination of the velocity of air in ducts is the

   22.____

    A. psychrometer
    C. U gauge
    B. pitot tube
    D. spherometer

23. A high tension breaker (4160 volts) should be equipped with a mechanical interlock which will prevent the breaker from being raised or advanced into, and lowered or withdrawn from, the operating position UNLESS

   23.____

    A. it is open
    B. it is closed
    C. the full load is connected
    D. a light load is connected

24. The proper fire extinguishing agent to use to extinguish fires in electrical equipment is

   24.____

    A. water
    C. soda-acid
    B. foam
    D. carbon dioxide

25. Direct current motors, for best performance, should have their brushes set on the commutator

   25.____

    A. at the neutral point (under load)
    B. at the point of maximum armature reaction
    C. radially at an angle of $90°$ (leading)
    D. radially at an angle of $80°$ (leading)

26. The PROPER order of events that take place in a 4-stroke cycle diesel engine is   26._____

     A. air intake, power expansion, compression, and exhaust
     B. air intake, compression, power, expansion, and exhaust
     C. power expansion, air intake, compression, and exhaust
     D. compression, air intake, power expansion, and exhaust

27. The one of the following lubricants which is LEAST likely to be attacked by acids is   27._____

     A. cottonseed oil   B. castor oil
     C. rapeseed oil   D. graphite

28. In general, non-rising steam gate valves are BEST adaptable for   28._____

     A. use where frequent adjustments are necessary
     B. installations carrying viscous liquids
     C. throttling or close control
     D. places where space is a factor

29. The presence of moisture in insulating oil is undesirable. The percentage of moisture which will reduce the dielectric strength of insulating oil to approximately one-half of its dielectric strength when dry is MOST NEARLY _____ % of moisture.   29._____

     A. 0.5   B. 0.05   C. 0.005   D. 0.0005

30. It has been brought to your attention that one of the men under your supervision is complaining to fellow co-workers that another man has received an easy assignment through his *connections*.
In this situation, it is BEST to   30._____

     A. privately inform the man who is complaining of the truth regarding the assignment
     B. in the presence of others, demand absolute proof from the man who is complaining
     C. ignore the matter since it is not your job to interfere in disagreements between the men
     D. tell the complaining man to apply for a desirable assignment also

KEY (CORRECT ANSWERS)

1.	B	16.	C
2.	A	17.	D
3.	D	18.	C
4.	D	19.	A
5.	B	20.	B
6.	D	21.	A
7.	C	22.	B
8.	B	23.	C
9.	B	24.	D
10.	A	25.	C
11.	C	26.	B
12.	A	27.	D
13.	A	28.	D
14.	C	29.	C
15.	D	30.	A

TEST 2

DIRECTIONS: Each question or incomplete statement is followed by several suggested answers or completions. Select the one that BEST answers the question or completes the statement. *PRINT THE LETTER OF THE CORRECT ANSWER IN THE SPACE AT THE RIGHT.*

1. The direction of rotation of a DC shunt motor can be reversed by reversing the   1._____

   A. line leads
   B. armature *and* field current
   C. field *or* armature current
   D. current in one pole winding

2. The insulation resistance of the stator winding of an induction motor is MOST commonly measured or tested with a(n)   2._____

   A. strobe   B. ammeter   C. megger   D. S-meter

3. Assume that three 12 ohm resistors are connected in delta across a 208 volt, 3-phase circuit.
The line current, in amperes, will be MOST NEARLY   3._____

   A. 30   B. 20.4   C. 17.32   D. 8.66

4. Assume that three 12 ohm resistors are connected in wye across a 208 volt, 3-phase circuit.
The power, in watts, dissipated in this resistance load will be MOST NEARLY   4._____

   A. 4200   B. 3600   C. 1200   D. 900

5. The one of the following knots which is MOST commonly used to shorten a rope without cutting it is the   5._____

   A. clove hitch   B. diamond knot
   C. sheepshank   D. square knot

6. Cast iron castings that need repairing are USUALLY repaired by the process known as   6._____

   A. electric arc welding   B. electro-forming
   C. resistance welding   D. brazing

7. The term SAE stands for   7._____

   A. Standard Auto Engines
   B. Standard Air Engines
   C. Society of Automotive Engineers
   D. Society of Aviation Engineers

8. The type of valve which is generally used where extremely close regulation of flow is needed is the _____ valve.   8._____

   A. gate   B. globe   C. needle   D. blow-off

9. Lubricating oils of mineral origin are refined from _____ products.　　9.____

  A. lard-beef   B. cottonseed
  C. crude petroleum   D. lime soap

10. The compression ratio of a diesel engine that has no starting ignition device is GENER-　　10.____
ALLY in the range of

  A. 11 to 20   B. 8 to 10   C. 6 to 8   D. 4 to 6

11. The base in a lubricating grease denotes the　　11.____

  A. type of soap used in its manufacture
  B. consistency and texture of the grease
  C. dropping or melting point of the grease
  D. residue content of the grease

12. Of the following sets of pipes, the one having a total combined area EXACTLY equal to　　12.____
the area of a 12" diameter pipe is _____ 6" pipes and _____ 8" pipes.

  A. two; no   B. no; two   C. two; one   D. four; no

13. If rubber gloves commonly used on high tension work are found on testing to have pin-　　13.____
holes, they

  A. may be used on low voltage
  B. should be discarded
  C. should be patched with rubber tape
  D. may be used only in dry places

14. Of the following types of soap-based greases, the one which has a fibrous texture is　　14.____

  A. calcium   B. sodium   C. aluminum   D. lithium

15. Of the following types of soap-based greases, the one that is BEST for lubricating plain　　15.____
bearings and line shafting is

  A. calcium   B. sodium   C. aluminum   D. lithium

16. One of the difficult features of steam turbine lubrication is　　16.____

  A. extreme oil pressure required
  B. emulsification of the oil
  C. excessive acidity or alkalinity of available oils
  D. limitation on the size of oil coolers

17. The rate of oil feed to a steam engine is USUALLY specified in　　17.____

  A. saybolt universal seconds
  B. capacity per running time
  C. pints per hour
  D. drops per minute

18. The grade of oil GENERALLY used to lubricate a worm gear is SAE　　18.____

  A. 20   B. 30   C. 50   D. 140

19. The distinguishing characteristic of steam-engine cylinder oil is   19.____

    A. a high flash point   B. a low flash point
    C. its color   D. its oiliness

20. Degrees Baume is a measure of fuel oil   20.____

    A. temperature   B. viscosity
    C. density   D. flash and fire point

21. How does cylinder oil compare with engine oil at room temperature?   21.____
Cylinder oil

    A. is lighter in color
    B. has a higher viscosity
    C. has a lower viscosity
    D. is lighter when put in front of a light

22. For the operation of a high tension breaker (4160 volts), the suitable control voltage for   22.____
BEST performance is

    A. 600 volts AC   B. 600 volts DC
    C. 208 to 440 volts AC   D. 70 to 140 volts DC

23. The equipment on which you would be MOST likely to find an unloader is a(n)   23.____

    A. centrifugal water pump   B. air compressor
    C. vacuum pump   D. steam engine

24. The term Saybolt refers to a measure of   24.____

    A. specific gravity   B. boiling point
    C. hardness   D. viscosity

25. Assume that a centrifugal fan running at 750 rpm delivers 20,000 cfm at a static pressure   25.____
of one inch.
If this fan is required to deliver 28,000 cfm at the same static pressure, it should be run
at a speed, in rpm, of MOST NEARLY

    A. 1500   B. 1250   C. 1150   D. 1050

26. The horsepower of a fan varies as the _____ of the fan speed.   26.____

    A. cube   B. square
    C. square root   D. cube root

27. The gearing for transmitting power between two shafts at right angles to each other con-   27.____
sists of two essential parts:

    A. two worm wheels   B. a worm and bevel gear
    C. a rack and pinion   D. two bevel gears

28. If a transmission main drive gear, having 30 teeth, rotates at 400 rpm and drives a coun-   28.____
tershaft drive gear at 300 rpm, the total number of teeth on the countershaft drive gear
will be

    A. 30   B. 40   C. 60   D. 80

29. The one of the following faults of a circuit breaker main contact which is NOT a cause of overheating of air circuit breakers is   29.____

    A. excessive pressure
    B. insufficient area in contact
    C. oxidized contacts
    D. dirty contacts

30. Of the following ranges of oil viscosities, the range MOST suitable for the lubrication of both cylinders and bearings of a reciprocating water cooled compressor, in Saybolt Universal seconds at 100° F is   30.____

    A. 10-110   B. 100-200   C. 300-400   D. 600-700

KEY (CORRECT ANSWERS)

1.	A	16.	B
2.	C	17.	D
3.	C	18.	C
4.	B	19.	A
5.	C	20.	C
6.	D	21.	B
7.	C	22.	D
8.	C	23.	B
9.	C	24.	D
10.	A	25.	D
11.	C	26.	A
12.	D	27.	D
13.	B	28.	B
14.	B	29.	A
15.	A	30.	B

EXAMINATION SECTION

TEST 1

DIRECTIONS: Each question or incomplete statement is followed by several suggested answers or completions. Select the one that BEST answers the question or completes the statement. *PRINT THE LETTER OF THE CORRECT ANSWER IN THE SPACE AT THE RIGHT.*

1. The MAIN advantage of a rotary pump over a centrifugal pump is that it   1._____
   A. has more velocity
   B. has greater speed
   C. delivers more gallons per minute
   D. is self-priming and requires no valves

2. Pump efficiency can be termed   2._____
   I. hydraulic   II. volumetric   III. thermal   IV. mechanical

   The CORRECT answer is:
   A. I, II   B. I, III, IV   C. I, II, IV   D. I, II, III, IV

3. A superheater vent valve is installed on a boiler to   3._____
   A. insure a flow of steam through the superheater when steam is being raised on the boiler
   B. insure that some of the excess steam is released
   C. lower the steam temperature
   D. none of the above

4. Which of the following is a wearing ring on a centrifugal pump?   4._____
   A. Lantern   B. Turbine   C. Impeller   D. Thrust

5. Worn sealing rings can cause the   5._____
   A. capacity to increase
   B. discharge to flow back into the inlet
   C. priming to stop
   D. shaft to throw out of alignment

6. Vibration is caused by   6._____
   A. packing too tight   B. water hammer
   C. shaft alignment   D. worn bearings

7. A condensate pump helps to   7._____
   A. create vacuum in the system
   B. induce the steam to circulate rapidly
   C. return the condensate back to the boiler
   D. reduce the back pressure on the engine

8. Important pumps on a feedwater line are the   8.._____
   I. rotary   II. vacuum   III. turbine   IV. centrifugal
   The CORRECT answer is:
   A. I, II   B. II, III, IV   C. I, II, III   D. I, II, III, IV

9. Which of the following is a reciprocating pump?   9._____
    A. Two stage   B. Turbine
    C. Simplex   D. All of the above

10. Which cylinder is larger on a duplex pump?   10._____
    A. Water   B. Air
    C. Steam   D. All are the same size

11. The FEWEST number of valves on a duplex pump is   11._____
    A. 4   B. 8   C. 12   D. 16

12. A pump may fail to discharge when the   12._____
    A. pump is not properly primed
    B. inlet valve is stuck
    C. valve seats are in bad condition
    D. all of the above

13. A pump may pound and vibrate because of   13._____
    A. air in the liquid
    B. a leaky inlet line
    C. excessive speed
    D. all of the above

14. If a pump races while increasing its output, the cause may be   14._____
    A. a leaky plunger
    B. a broken or stuck water valve
    C. an air leak
    D. not enough steam to move the piston

15. If the piston strikes the head of the cylinder, the cause would MOST probably be   15._____
    A. improper adjustment of the cushion valve
    B. cylinder rings are worn
    C. too much lap on the valves
    D. none of the above

16. To adjust the cushion valve, you should   16._____
    A. run the pump at full speed
    B. cut down the steam supply
    C. run the pump with a full load
    D. run the pump without a water load

17. If the pump lacks a cushion valve, you should   17._____
    A. lower the steam pressure
    B. adjust the lost motion enough to permit the pump to make a full stroke without striking
    C. adjust the piston rings
    D. adjust the back pressure valve

18. What condition would cause a piston to stop on dead center? 18._____
  A. The slide valve is worn
  B. There is not enough steam pressure
  C. There is too high of a head
  D. The cylinder shoulders are worn

19, Positive suction head is a condition present when the 19._____
  A. pump is located below the liquid supply
  B. pump is located between the boiler and the feedwater tank
  C. pump is located above the liquid supply
  D. water pressure is greater than the suction pressure

20. A centrifugal pump will most likely fail if 20._____
  A. the suction side of the pump is defective
  B. the discharge valve is closed
  C. wearing rings are worn
  D. strainer is clogged

21. The pump may fail to discharge if there is 21._____
  A. not enough water pressure
  B. improper priming
  C. air trapped at the top of the casing causing the pump to lose its discharge
  D. too high of a head

22. The failure of a pump to discharge can be rectified by 22._____
  A. increasing the water pressure
  B. reducing the pipe size
  C. decreasing the water pressure
  D. repriming the pump

23. To prevent a pump from failing to discharge, you should 23._____
  A. install a lantern ring
  B. replace the impeller
  C. install a bigger motor
  D. remove some packing

24. Reduction in both capacity and head is caused by 24._____
  A. too much air leaking through the packing
  B. reverse rotation of the motor
  C. a closed suction valve
  D. a clogged strainer

25. Small by-pass lines are installed around a large gate valve in order to 25._____
  A. equalize the pressure on the globe valve
  B. balance the pressure on the gate valve when the valve is being opened
  C. increase the velocity of the steam
  D. eliminate the sudden change in temperature of the steam

―――――

KEY (CORRECT ANSWERS)

1.	D	11.	B
2.	D	12.	D
3.	A	13.	D
4.	C	14.	D
5.	B	15.	A
6.	D	16.	D
7.	C	17.	B
8.	D	18.	A
9.	C	19.	A
10.	C	20.	A

21.	B
22.	D
23.	A
24.	B
25.	B

———

TEST 2

DIRECTIONS: Each question or incomplete statement is followed by several suggested answers or completions. Select the one that BEST answers the question or completes the statement. *PRINT THE LETTER OF THE CORRECT ANSWER IN THE SPACE AT THE RIGHT.*

1. The purpose of a volume casing on a centrifugal pump is to   1._____
   A. convert velocity into vacuum
   B. convert velocity into pressure
   C. prevent cavitation of the pump
   D. increase the velocity of the water

2. How many type of feedwater heaters are currently in existence   2._____
   A. 1   B. 2   C. 4   D. 5

3. Which of the following are types of feedwater heaters?   3._____
   A. Economizer   B. Closed   C. Deaerator   D. All of the above

4. When the temperature leaving the feedwater heater is too low, the MAIN problem is   4._____
   probably that
   A. steam pressure is too low
   B. back pressure is too low
   C. steam is of poor quality
   D. too much condensate is in the steam

5. The advantage of a feedwater heater is: 5._____
   A. Hotter feedwater
   B. Less fuel consumption
   C. Less air in the feedwater
   D. All of the above

6. To increase the back pressure, you should   6._____
   A. install a bigger back pressure valve
   B. put a heavier spring on the valve
   C. close the back pressure valve
   D. increase the line pressure

7. Which of the following is NOT a use of a feedwater heater? To   7._____
   A. pre-heat the feedwater
   B. eliminate scale foaming substances by precipitation
   C. utilize some of the steam going to waste
   D. store generated steam

8. In relation to the feedwater pump, the feedwater heater should be located   8._____
   in another part of the building
   A. in the basement of the plant
   B. about 10 or 12 feet above the pump

9. An open feedwater heater is a heater   9._____
     A. open at one end
     B. with steam coils
     C. where water and steam are in actual contact
     D. with 2/3 steam space

10. The MAIN advantage of an open heater is that it   10._____
     A. can separate scale forming substances from the feed-water by precipitation
     B. produces hotter water
     C. can hold more steam
     D. is cheap to operate

11. How much steam supply is sufficient for an open heater?   11._____
     A. 3 to 5 lbs.   B. 5 to 7 lbs.   C. 8 to 10 lbs.   D. All of the above

12. _____ A(n)   should be installed on an open feedwater heater   12._____
     A. exhaust or vent pipe   B. oil separator
     C. steam gauge   D. all of the above

13. A closed feedwater heater is a heater in which   13._____
     A. steam travels through coils or tubes and water on the outside of the coils
     B. water runs through a tube with steam on the outside heating the water
     C. feedwater is heated and passed back to the deaerator
     D. none of the above

14. At what pressure should a feedwater heater operate?   14._____
     A. 1-15 lbs.   B. 15-20 lbs.   C. 20-25 lbs.   D. 25-30 lbs.

15. The safety device normally installed on a feedwater heater is a _____ valve.   15._____
     A. pneumatic   B. pressure relief
     C. safety   D. by-pass

16. The FIRST indication of a broken coil on a feedwater heater would be the   16._____
     A. heater filling up with water
     B. relief valve opening
     C. steam pressure increasing
     D. water pressure rising

17. On a double-acting reciprocating pump, what is installed on the discharge side of the pump? A(n)   17._____
     A. air chamber and gauge
     B. pressure gauge and relief valve.
     C. pressure gauge and safety valve
     D. air chamber and a gate valve

18. What types of lubricators are MOST commonly used today?   18._____
     I. Hydrokinetic   II. Force feed pump
     III. Splash system   IV. Gravity

     The CORRECT answer is:
     A. I, II   B. II, III, IV   C. I, III, IV   D. I, II, III, IV

19. What type of lubricant is used on piston rods and valve stems on a reciprocating pump?   19.____
    Mineral oil
    A. Compress oil
    B. Oil with high velocity
    C. Cylinder oil and graphite mixed together
    D. A reciprocating pump contains the following notation:

20. What is the diameter of the liquid cylinder? 7 x 6 x 4.   20._____
    A. 6"   B. 4"
    C. 7"   D. none of the above

21. What types of pumps are used in a heating system?   21._____
    I. Reciprocating   II. Condensate
    III, Centrifugal   IV. Vacuum

    The CORRECT answer is:
    A. I, II   B. I, III
    C. II, IV   D. III, IV

22. The purpose of a steam loop, or thermal pump, is to   22._____
    A. deliver steam to the engine
    B. protect water from entering the steam gauge
    C. return condensate back to the boiler
    D. trap steam from high pressure lines into a low-pressure line

23. What effect does a short stroke have on a reciprocating pump? It   23._____
    A. increases the pump capacity
    B. increases the steam capacity, and decreases the pump consumption
    C. increases the steam Consumption, and decreases the pump capacity
    D. relieves the pressure in the air chamber

24. A pump with two liquid cylinders, and one steam cylinder is called a pump.   24._____
    A. triplex   B. duplex
    C. tandem   D. double tandem

25. The air chamber on a reciprocating pump is located on the   25._____
    A. discharge side of the feed pump
    B. discharge side of the reciprocating pump
    C. discharge side of all pumps
    D. suction side of a reciprocating pump

_____

KEY (CORRECT ANSWERS)

1.	A	11.	D
2.	B	12.	D
3.	D	13.	A
4.	B	14.	A
5.	D	15.	B
6.	C	16.	B
7.	D	17.	B
8.	D	18.	D
9.	C	19.	D
10.	C	20.	A

21.	C
22.	C
23.	B
24.	C
25.	B

———

EXAMINATION SECTION
TEST 1

DIRECTIONS: Each question or incomplete statement is followed by several suggested answers or completions. Select the one that BEST answers the question or completes the Statement. *PRINT THE LETTER OF THE CORRECT ANSWER IN THE SPACE AT THE RIGHT.*

1. What type of pump has a diffusion *ring?*

    A. Centrifugal   B. Duplex double acting
    C. Helical gear   D. Spur gear

1.____

2. A cause of excessive oil consumption in an air compressor is

    A. oil with improper viscosity
    B. defective discharge valve
    C. oil level too high in oil sump
    D. loose unloader unit

2.____

3. How does cylinder oil compare with engine oil at engine room temperature? Cylinder oil

    A. is lighter in color
    B. has a higher viscosity
    C. has a lower viscosity
    D. is lighter when put in front of a light

3.____

4. On a boiler-feed centrifugal pump, to maintain a certain speed, 60 horsepower is used. To double that speed, so as to obtain double the output, how much horsepower is needed?

    A. 120   B. 240   C. 360   D. 480

4.____

5. The *slip* of a pump refers to

    A. lost motion on the steam slide valve
    B. leakage past the plunger on an outside packed pump
    C. recirculation of liquid from discharge side back to suction side
    D. clearance when piston is slipped inside cylinder

5.____

6. On a reciprocating vacuum pump, the diameter of the steam piston is _____ the liquid piston.

    A. larger than   B. smaller than
    C. the same size as   D. twice the diameter of

6.____

7. How many valves are there on the water end of a duplex double-acting feed pump?

    A. 8   B. 6   C. 4   D. 2

7.____

8. Which of the following would you find on a duplex pump? 8.____

    A. Springs and packing
    B. Gears and impeller
    C. Flywheel and crank
    D. Crankshaft and air chamber

9. The function of the air chamber on a duplex, double-acting pump is to 9.____

    A. prevent hammering
    B. increase capacity of pump
    C. aerate the water
    D. prevent cavitation

10. The valve discs on the water end of a duplex pump are USUALLY made of 10.____

    A. wood   B. steel
    C. rubber   D. cast iron

11. A direct-acting, duplex steam pump *short strokes* when it returns from overhaul. The PROBABLE cause is 11.____

    A. feed water too cold
    B. steam pressure too low
    C. steam valves not properly set
    D. water discharge pressure too high

12. A heavy duty pump is one which 12.____

    A. is designed for the pumping of heavy liquids
    B. pumps large quantities of water
    C. has a high thermal efficiency
    D. is made of extra heavy material for high head pressure

13. When a punch is used in making holes for rivets or boiler tubes, the diameter of the punch shall be _____ the desired hole. 13.____

    A. three-quarters of the diameter of
    B. slightly smaller than
    C. exactly the same size as
    D. slightly larger than

14. On a _____ pump, you would find a *volute*. 14.____

    A. reciprocating   B. centrifugal
    C. jet   D. direct-pressure

15. In starting a centrifugal boiler feed pump with 300 lbs. water pressure on the line, the valves should be set with suction _____ and discharge _____. 15.____

    A. open; open   B. open; closed
    C. closed; closed   D. closed; open

16. On a centrifugal boiler feed pump, the regulating valve functions to maintain 16.____

    A. speed constant   B. pressure constant
    C. variable speed   D. water level

17. With centrifugal pumps, the head varies directly as the   17.____

    A. speed   B. speed squared
    C. speed cubed   D. diameter squared

18. An intercooler is used on a   18.____

    A. compound engine   B. two-stage air compressor
    C. two-stage turbine   D. two-stage evactor

19. The unloader on an air compressor is provided for   19.____

    A. reducing pressure   B. easy starting
    C. high-starting pressure   D. reducing temperature

20. A duplex center outside a packed feed water pump has   20.____

    A. yoke rod   B. two water plungers
    C. compound steam glands   D. four water pistons

21. A centrifugal pump operates with a high suction lift, which would require _____ line.   21.____

    A. lift check at bottom of suction
    B. swing check in discharge
    C. stop valve in discharge
    D. lift check at top of suction

22. Diffuser vanes will MOST generally be found in a _____ pump.   22.____

    A. centrifugal turbine   B. centrifugal volute
    C. rotary   D. reciprocating

23. A sewer ejector would be located   23.____

    A. on the roof of a building
    B. in the basement
    C. in the sub-basement
    D. in the sewer

24. How many pots are there on a double-acting water pump?   24.____

    A. 1   B. 2   C. 3   D. 4

25. What is the amount of steam consumption of a simple, duplex steam pump, in lbs./H.P. hour?   25.____

    A. 5-20   B. 25-35   C. 50-90   D. 120-200

KEY (CORRECT ANSWERS)

1.	A	11.	C
2.	C	12.	D
3.	B	13.	D
4.	D	14.	B
5.	B	15.	A
6.	B	16.	D
7.	A	17.	B
8.	A	18.	B
9.	A	19.	A
10.	C	20.	B

21.	A
22.	A
23.	C
24.	D
25.	A

TEST 2

DIRECTIONS: Each question or incomplete statement is followed by several suggested answers or completions. Select the one that BEST answers the question or completes the statement. *PRINT THE LETTER OF THE CORRECT ANSWER IN THE SPACE AT THE RIGHT.*

1. The type of valve on a duplex steam pump is
   1.____

   A. sleeve   B. piston
   C. D-slide valve   D. poppet

2. The slide valve on a Knowles pump is operated by
   2.____

   A. linkage attached to the piston rod
   B. rocker arm of opposite steam slide
   C. an auxiliary piston
   D. discharge water pressure

3. A duplex, double-acting pump with the valves properly adjusted will
   3.____

   A. not start sometimes
   B. always start
   C. jig
   D. start when off dead center

4. If one valve stem of a duplex, double-acting pump broke, the pump would
   4.____

   A. increase in speed   B. run slower
   C. stop   D. run on one side only

5. The diameter of the steam cylinders of an 18 x 16 x 24 duplex, direct-acting steam pump is _____ inches.
   5.____

   A. 18   B. 16   C. 24   D. 30

6. On a boiler feed pump, the
   6.____

   A. steam cylinder is always larger than the water cylinder
   B. water cylinder is always larger than the steam cylinder
   C. cylinders are of equal size
   D. water discharge pipe is always larger than the suction pipe

7. Flax packing is used for
   7.____

   A. steam end of pump
   B. water end of pump
   C. between flanges of pipe lines
   D. high temperature

8. Water is dripping out of the gland of a centrifugal pump used to pump feed water. You should
   8.____

   A. renew the packing at the first opportunity
   B. pull up the gland as tight as possible with an ordinary 6 inch pipe wrench

C.   pull up the gland just to the point where water does not leak out
D.   do nothing

9.   On the initial tightening of a jam-type gland on a boiler-feed water pump to stop exces-
     sive leakage, you would pull up alternately on the hexagonal nuts _____ turn.

     A.   1/6   B.   1/2   C.   3/4   D.   1 full

10. Diffuser vanes will MOST generally be found in a _____ pump.

     A.   centrifugal turbine   B.   centrifugal volute
     C.   rotary   D.   reciprocating

11. If the consumption of lubricating oil in an air compressor is excessive, it is MOST likely
     due to

     A.   using too high viscosity oil
     B.   a defective discharge valve
     C.   a loose unloader unit
     D.   oil too high in sump

12. Which of the following statements is CORRECT about a Worthington steam-driven
     duplex double-acting boiler feed pump?

     A.   Will always start in position in which it was stopped
     B.   Will not start if stopped with one piston at extreme head end and other at dead
          center
     C.   Speed is controlled by inertia type governor
     D.   Dust of f must always be 25%

13. Centrifugal boiler feed pumps for large boilers with fluctuating loads are usually fitted with
     a system for recirculating or recycling.
     This is done to prevent

     A.   excessive head pressure
     B.   loss of suction
     C.   excessing governor action
     D.   overheating with consequent flashing and seizing of the pump

14. In the operation of a turbo-driven centrifugal pump, the delivery of the pump would
     PROPERLY be controlled by

     A.   throttling the discharge
     B.   throttling the suction
     C.   using a bypass
     D.   throttling the steam supply

15. Assume that it is necessary to pump 40 M.G.D. against a 65 ft. head.
     If the pump efficiency is 65%, the B.H.P. of this pump is MOST NEARLY

     A.   920   B.   700   C.   460   D.   176

9._____

10._____

11._____

12._____

13._____

14._____

15._____

16. Assume that a pump had to be shut down temporarily due to trouble which was first reported by an oiler.
The one of the following entries in the log concerning this occurrence which is LEAST important is

    A. time of the shutdown
    B. period of time the pump was out of service
    C. cause of the trouble
    D. time the oiler came on shift

17. At sea level, the theoretical maximum distance, in feet, the water can be lifted by suction *only* is MOST NEARLY

    A. 12.00   B. 14.70   C. 33.57   D. 72.00

18. While a lubricating oil is in use, for good performance, its neutralization number should

    A. keep rising   B. remain about the same
    C. be greater than 0.1   D. be greater than 2.0

19. The parts of a large sewage pump that would MOST likely need repairs after the fewest number of hours of operation are the

    A. pump casings   B. impellers
    C. wearing rings   D. outboard bearings

20. Flexible coupling used to connect a pump to an electric motor valve is USUALLY rated in horsepower per

    A. 100 rpm of shaft
    B. 300 rpm of shaft
    C. square inch of shaft area
    D. inch of shaft diameter

KEY (CORRECT ANSWERS)

1. C	11. D
2. B	12. A
3. B	13. D
4. C	14. D
5. A	15. B
6. A	16. D
7. B	17. C
8. D	18. B
9. A	19. C
10. A	20. A

EXAMINATION SECTION
TEST 1

DIRECTIONS: Each question or incomplete statement is followed by several suggested answers or completions. Select the one that BEST answers the question or completes the statement. *PRINT THE LETTER OF THE CORRECT ANSWER IN THE SPACE AT THE RIGHT.*

1. The flow of sewage into the treatment plant is USUALLY controlled by a   1.____

   A. gate valve   B. sluice gate
   C. tainter gate   D. parshall gate

2. Regulator gates USUALLY close when the sewage in the interceptor sewer reaches a   2.____
   predetermined

   A. velocity   B. pressure
   C. temperature   D. elevation

3. A bar screen serves the same purpose as a   3.____

   A. filter   B. grit collector
   C. trash rack   D. sluice gate

4. Material that is removed from the sewage by the fine screen is MOST frequently   4.____

   A. blown by compressed air to the grit storage tank
   B. ground up and returned to the sewage
   C. burnt as fuel for the plant
   D. dried in the sludge drying beds and then disposed at sea

5. The one of the following pieces of equipment that is operated in conjunction with air pres-   5.____
   sure is a(n)

   A. centrifugal pump   B. venturi
   C. ejector   D. sump pump

6. One of the methods used to prime a centrifugal pump is to   6.____

   A. raise the air pressure in the pump
   B. bleed the suction line
   C. apply a vacuum to the pump
   D. open the suction valve

7. The one of the following types of pumps MOST frequently used to pump thickened   7.____
   sludge is the _____ type.

   A. ejector   B. centrifugal
   C. gear   D. piston

8. A plant is called an *Activated Sludge Plant* when the   8.____

   A. thickened sludge can be used as fertilizer
   B. gases from the sludge digestion tanks are burnt as fuel
   C. sludge must be dried before being disposed
   D. partly treated sewage is mixed with sludge

9. Where a digester tank has either a floating or a rising cover, it is made airtight by means of a(n)

    A. water seal   B. sliding rubber gasket
    C. leather *bellows*   D. oiled steel ring

9.____

10. Grease and fats are USUALLY removed from the sewage by

    A. skimming the liquid in the sedimentation tanks
    B. pumping the liquid from the sump in the grit chamber
    C. decanting the liquid in the digestion tank
    D. backwashing the fine screens

10.____

11. The type of plant in which *flocculation* MOST frequently occurs is the _____ plant.

    A. aerated sludge   B. chemical precipitation
    C. plain screening   D. filtration

11.____

12. Chlorine leaks are BEST detected by use of

    A. orthotoludin   B. litmus paper
    C. ammonia   D. copperas

12.____

13. Settling tanks operate effectively by _____ the sewage.

    A. slowing the speed of
    B. increasing the speed of
    C. changing the direction of flow of
    D. adding air to

13.____

14. A *venturi* is used in a sewage treatment plant in order to

    A. clean the diffusers
    B. control the amount of sewage in the wet well
    C. measure the flow of sewage
    D. reduce the pressure of the gases used as fuel

14.____

15. Sludge tanks are USUALLY heated by means of

    A. forced warm air   B. hot water
    C. radiant heat   D. electric coils

15.____

16. Chlorine is USUALLY added to sewage by

    A. adding the gas directly to the sewage
    B. mixing a small quantity of the sewage with the chlorine and then adding the mixture to the main body of sewage
    C. mixing the chlorine with water, and then adding the mixture to the sewage
    D. combining the gas with the air used in the aeration tank

16.____

17. The MAIN reason for defective operation of an aeration tank is that

    A. sewage flow is too slow
    B. of clogged diffuser plates
    C. tank temperature is too low
    D. too much air is supplied

17.____

18. The type of pump that seldom requires a relief valve is MOST likely a _____ pump. 18.____

    A. reciprocating   B. gear
    C. piston   D. centrifugal

19. The MAIN purpose of a foot valve in a centrifugal pump is to 19.____

    A. prevent the liquid from flowing back down the suction line
    B. equalize the pressure on both sides of the pump
    C. make it easier to prime the pump
    D. block passage of material that is too large to pump

20. The MAIN reason for lubricating machinery is to 20.____

    A. lower operating temperature
    B. keep down noise and vibration
    C. reduce friction
    D. lower cost of operation

21. The one of the following items that has the LOWEST viscosity is 21.____

    A. cup grease   B. kerosene
    C. #10 oil   D. #40 oil

22. The one of the following statements that is MOST NEARLY correct is: 22.____

    A. High speed machinery is most frequently lubricated by grease
    B. For most applications, either grease or oil can be used
    C. When in doubt, it is best to use the heavier of two grades of oil available
    D. Oil becomes *thinner* as the operating temperature increases

23. The function of a circuit breaker is MOST similar to that of a 23.____

    A. switch   B. fuse   C. rheostat   D. transformer

24. Noisy operation of a motor is MOST frequently caused by 24.____

    A. a shorted armature   B. over-voltage
    C. worn bearings   D. a grounded casing

25. Consumption of electrical energy is registered on a(n) 25.____

    A. volt-ohm meter   B. ammeter
    C. watt-hour meter   D. ohm meter

26. A dirty commutator is BEST cleaned by using 26.____

    A. sandpaper   B. soap and water
    C. emery cloth   D. kerosene

27. The one of the following items that is MOST frequently used to prevent an electric motor from being overloaded is a 27.____

    A. warning signal   B. governor
    C. thermal cut-out   D. rheostat

28. The one of the following metals that is MOST commonly used for outboard bearings is 28.____

    A. zinc   B. brass   C. magnesium   D. babbit

29. The use of pipe joint compound when making up a screwed joint results in a watertight joint and also   29.____

    A. cleans the threads
    B. makes the joint hard
    C. lubricates the threads
    D. prevents cross threading

30. A pipe is generally threaded by using a   30.____

    A. die
    B. tap
    C. yoke
    D. swedge

31. The type of motor that MOST frequently does NOT use brushes is the   31.____

    A. universal type
    B. series wound D.C. motor
    C. synchronous motor
    D. induction motor

32. Compressed air can be used to clean generator and motor windings provided the air is   32.____

    A. heated
    B. blown at a high velocity
    C. used at a pressure of at least 90 lbs./sq.in.
    D. dry

33. The use of a cold chisel with a *mushroomed* head is   33.____

    A. *good*, because the mushrooming cushions the blow
    B. *bad*, because the head cannot be hit squarely
    C. *good*, because there is more area on the head to hit
    D. *bad*, because chips might fly from the head

34. After brass or black iron pipe has been cut, it should be   34.____

    A. counterbored
    B. reamed
    C. countersunk
    D. squared

35. The one of the following that is used to change the speed of certain types of electric motors is a (n)   35.____

    A. commutator
    B. brush
    C. rheostat
    D. armature

36. The type of pipe that is MOST frequently made with bell and spigot ends is   36.____

    A. brass
    B. steel
    C. cast iron
    D. transite

37. The one of the following that is used to connect two pipes together in a straight line is a   37.____

    A. manifold
    B. divider
    C. band
    D. union

38. The difference between a stud and a bolt is that the stud has   38.____

    A. a finer thread
    B. no head
    C. a round head
    D. a coarser thread

39. A set screw is often used to 39.____

    A. bolt two pieces of flanged pipe together
    B. screw together matching parts in a motor casing
    C. clamp a piece to a work table
    D. secure a pulley to a shaft

40. Soft jaw inserts sometimes used to protect the surface of a piece of metal that is held in 40.____
    a vise are MOST frequently made of

    A. zinc   B. tin   C. brass   D. pewter

41. The BEST type of wrench to use on a large square nut is a _____ wrench. 41.____

    A. monkey   B. spanner   C. stillson   D. spintite

42. The BEST method of cleaning files is to use a 42.____

    A. file card   B. knife
    C. scriber   D. fibre brush

43. The BEST lubricant to use when cutting threads on steel pipe is _____ oil. 43.____

    A. pike   B. penetrating
    C. lard   D. coal

44. The BEST type of valve to use to control the flow of liquid to a delicate gauge is a _____ 44.____
    valve.

    A. gate   B. needle   C. globe   D. check

45. Water hammer is caused MAINLY by 45.____

    A. pumping sewage to too high a head
    B. interrupting the flow of sewage too rapidly
    C. debris floating in the sewage
    D. excessive corrosion in the pipes

46. Suppose a centrifugal pump is pumping less sewage than it is capable of handling. 46.____
    Of the following, the one that is NOT a possible reason for this is that the

    A. speed of pump is too slow
    B. pump is not properly primed
    C. stuffing box packing is defective
    D. suction line is partly clogged

47. The one of the following types of pumps that will give a smooth continuous flow of liquid 47.____
    rather than a pulsating flow is the _____ type.

    A. reciprocating   B. rotary
    C. gear   D. centrifugal

48. For pumping against a very high head, the BEST type of pump to use is a _____ type. 48.____

    A. reciprocating   B. propeller
    C. mixed flow   D. centrifugal

49. To increase the volume of delivery of a reciprocating pump, USUALLY the   49.____

    A. angle of the impeller is increased
    B. inlet valve is opened wider
    C. piston stroke is lengthened
    D. discharge valve is opened wider

50. The capacity of a pump is MOST frequently expressed in   50.____

    A. cubic feet per day   B. gallons per day
    C. cubic feet per minute   D. gallons per minute

KEY (CORRECT ANSWERS)

1.	B	11.	B	21.	B	31.	D	41.	A
2.	D	12.	C	22.	D	32.	D	42.	A
3.	C	13.	A	23.	B	33.	D	43.	C
4.	B	14.	C	24.	C	34.	B	44.	B
5.	C	15.	B	25.	C	35.	C	45.	B
6.	C	16.	C	26.	A	36.	C	46.	B
7.	D	17.	B	27.	C	37.	D	47.	D
8.	D	18.	D	28.	D	38.	B	48.	A
9.	A	19.	A	29.	C	39.	D	49.	C
10.	A	20.	C	30.	A	40.	C	50.	D

TEST 2

DIRECTIONS: Each question or incomplete statement is followed by several suggested answers or completions. Select the one that BEST answers the question or completes the statement. *PRINT THE LETTER OF THE CORRECT ANSWER IN THE SPACE AT THE RIGHT.*

1. The sum of the following dimensions: 1 5/8, 2 1/4, 4 1/16, 3 3/16, is

   A. 10 15/16   B. 11   C. 11 1/8   D. 11 1/4

   1._____

2. Assume that six men, working together at the same rate of speed, can complete a certain job in 3 hours.
   If, however, there were only four men available to do this job, and they all worked at the same rate of speed, to complete this job would take MOST NEARLY _____ hours.

   A. 4 1/4   B. 4 1/2   C. 4 3/4   D. 5

   2._____

3. Due to unforeseen difficulties, a job which would normally take 17 hours to complete was actually completed in 21 hours.
   This represents a percent increase over the normal time of MOST NEARLY

   A. 19%   B. 2.4%   C. 24%   D. 124%

   3._____

4. The veteran should approach the problem of safety with the idea that

   A. there will always be accidents
   B. most accidents can be prevented
   C. the best method of preventing accidents is to post safety rules for the men to follow
   D. punishing the man with the worst accident record will reduce the number of accidents occurring

   4._____

5. The one of the following that is NOT a common cause of accidents occurring when working around machinery is

   A. wearing loose clothing
   B. wearing gloves
   C. having insufficient illumination
   D. having slippery floors

   5._____

Questions 6-8.

DIRECTIONS: Questions 6 through 8, inclusive, are to be answered in accordance with the following information.
   A certain job requires 4 men working the number of hours and at the salary rate indicated in the accompanying table.

Name	No. of Hours	Salary/Hr.
Brown	30	$15.00
Jones	22	$19.50
Walter	40	$10.50
Thomas	25	$17.22

6. According to the above table, the salary received by Thomas on this job is MOST
NEARLY

    A. $426.00   B. $427.50   C. $429.00   D. $430.50

6.____

7. According to the above table, the man who received the MOST wages chargeable to this
job is

    A. Brown   B. Jones   C. Walter   D. Thomas

7.____

8. According to the above table, the total amount of wages chargeable to this job is MOST
NEARLY

    A. $1,726.50   B. $1,717.50   C. $1,729.50   D. $1,737.50

8.____

9. Of the following statements, the one that represents the SAFEST practice in a shop is:
Adjustments should be made on.

    A. running machinery only if another man can be assigned to guard the man making
        the actual adjustment
    B. running machinery only if proper protective equipment is worn
    C. running machinery only when the machine is grounded
    D. machinery only after the machine has been stopped

9.____

10. Regarding work performed on electrical circuits, the one of the following that is unsafe is
to

    A. use #10 wire instead of #12
    B. ground the junction boxes
    C. replace a 15 ampere circuit breaker with a 20 ampere one
    D. open the main switch before working on the wiring

10.____

11. Of the following, the MOST important reason for making detailed reports of all accidents
is to

    A. have a record of who to blame for the accident
    B. be able to properly assess the cost of the accident
    C. reduce the number of *compensation* claims
    D. determine the causes of accidents and eliminate future accidents

11.____

12. As a veteran sewage treatment worker, you can BEST promote safety in your operations
by

    A. carefully investigating and reporting the circumstances of any accident
    B. suggesting safer methods of operation
    C. training subordinates in proper safety
    D. disciplining subordinates who engage in unsafe acts

12.____

13. Oil-soaked rags are BEST stored in a

    A. neat pile in a readily accessible corner
    B. metal container with a tight cover
    C. metal box that has holes for adequate ventilation
    D. closet on a shelf above the ground

13.____

14. The one of the following actions that is NOT the cause of injury when working with hand tools is   14._____

    A. working with defective tools
    B. using the wrong tool for the job
    C. working too carefully
    D. using a tool improperly

15. Artificial respiration is the FIRST action you should take when a man becomes unconscious either as a result of drowning or as a result of   15._____

    A. chlorine poisoning   B. electric shock
    C. falling   D. clothing catching fire

Questions 16-17.

DIRECTIONS: Questions 16 and 17 should be answered in accordance with the following paragraph.

Sewage treatment plants are designed so that the sewage flow reaches the plant by gravity. In some instances, a small percentage of the sewerage system may be below the planned level of the plant. Economy in construction and other factors may indicate that the raising of that lower portion of the flow by means of pumps, to the desired plant elevation, is more desirable than lowering the plant structure. Some plants operate with this feature.

16. According to the above paragraph,   16._____

    A. a small percentage of the sewage reaches the plant by means of gravity
    B. all sewage reaches the plant by means of gravity
    C. where sewage cannot reach the plant by gravity it is pumped
    D. pumping is used so that all sewage can reach the plant

17. According to the above paragraph, the reason that some plants are built above the level of the sewerage system is that   17._____

    A. these plants operate more efficiently this way
    B. gravity will naturally bring the sewage in at a lower level
    C. pumping of the sewage is more expensive
    D. these plants are cheaper to build this way

Questions 18-20.

DIRECTIONS: Questions 18 through 20, inclusive, should be answered in accordance with the following paragraph.

Accident proneness is a subject which deserves much move objective and competent study than it has received to date. In discussing accident proneness, it is important to differentiate between the employee who is a "repeater" and one who is truly accident prone. It is obvious that any person put on work of which he knows little without thorough training in safe practice for the work in question will be liable to injury until he does learn the "how" of it. Few workmen left to their own devices will develop adequate safe practices. Therefore, they must be trained. Only those who fail to respond to proper training should be regarded as accident prone. The repeater whose accident record can be explained by a correctible physical defect, by correctible plant or machine hazards, by assignment to work for which he is not suited because of physical deficiencies or special abilities, cannot be fairly called "accident prone."

18. According to the above paragraph, a person is considered accident prone if

18.____

    A. he has accidents regardless of the fact that he has been properly trained
    B. he has many accidents
    C. it is possible for him to have accidents
    D. he works at a job where accidents are possible

19. According to the above paragraph,

19.____

    A. workers will learn the safe way of doing things if left to their own intelligence
    B. most workers must be trained to be safe
    C. a worker who has had more than one accident has not been properly trained
    D. intelligent workers are always safe

20. According to the above paragraph, a person would not be called accident prone if the cause of his accidents was

20.____

    A. a lack of interest in the job
    B. recklessness
    C. a low level of intelligence
    D. eyeglasses that don't fit properly

Questions 21-23.

DIRECTIONS: Questions 21 through 23, inclusive, should be answered in accordance with the following paragraph.

    Sharpening a twist drill by hand is a skill that is mastered only after much practice and careful attention to the details. Therefore, whenever possible, use a tool grinder in which the drills can be properly positioned, clamped in place, and set with precision for the various angles. This machine grinding will enable you to sharpen the drills accurately. As a result, they will last longer and will produce more accurate holes.

21. According to the above paragraph, one reason for sharpening drills accurately is that the drills

21.____

    A. can then be used in a hand drill as well as a drill press
    B. will last longer
    C. can then be used by unskilled persons
    D. cost less

22. According to the above paragraph,

22.____

    A. it is easier to sharpen a drill by machine than by hand
    B. drills cannot be sharpened by hand
    C. only a skilled mechanic can learn to sharpen a drill by hand
    D. a good mechanic will learn to sharpen drills by hand

23. As used in the above paragraph, the word *precision* means MOST NEARLY

23.____

    A. accuracy   B. ease   C. rigidity   D. speed

Questions 24-27.

DIRECTIONS: Questions 24 through 27, inclusive, should be answered in accordance with the following paragraph.

Centrifugal pumps have relatively fewer moving parts than reciprocating pumps, and no valves. While reciprocating pumps when new are usually more efficient than centrifugal pumps, the latter retain their efficiency longer. Most rotary pumps are also without valves, but they have closely meshed parts between which high pressures may be set up after they begin to wear. In general, centrifugal pumps can be made much smaller than reciprocating pumps giving the same result. There is an exception, in that positive displacement pumps delivering small volumes at high heads are smaller than equivalent centrifugal pumps. Centrifugal pumps cost less when first purchased than other comparable pumps. The original outlay may be as little as one-third or one-half that of a reciprocating pump suitable for the same purpose.

24.   The type of pump NOT mentioned in the above paragraph is the _____ type.   24.____

    A.   rotary   B.   propeller
    C.   reciprocating   D.   centrifugal

25.   According to the above paragraph, the type of pump that sometimes has valves and   25.____
sometimes does NOT is the

    A.   rotary   B.   propeller
    C.   reciprocating   D.   centrifugal

26.   According to the above paragraph, centrifugal pumps are   26.____

    A.   *always smaller* than reciprocating pumps
    B.   *smaller* than reciprocating pumps only when designed to deliver small quantities at low pressures
    C.   *larger* than reciprocating pumps only when designed to deliver small quantities at high pressures
    D.   *larger* than reciprocating pumps only when designed to deliver large quantities at low pressures

27.   The advantage of centrifugal pumps that is NOT mentioned in the above paragraph is   27.____
that

    A.   the centrifugal pump retains its efficiency longer
    B.   it is impossible to create an excessive pressure when using a centrifugal pump
    C.   there are fewer parts to wear out in a centifugal pump
    D.   the centrifugal pump is cheaper

Questions 28-30.

DIRECTIONS: Questions 28 through 30, inclusive, should be answered in accordance with the following paragraph.

Gaskets made of relatively soft materials are placed between the meeting surfaces of hydraulic fittings in order to increase the tightness of the seal. They should be composed of materials that will not be affected by the liquid to be enclosed, nor by the conditions under which the system operates, including maximum pressure and temperature. They should be able to maintain the amount of clearance required between meeting surfaces. One of the materials most widely used in making gaskets is neoprene. Since neoprene is flexible, it is often used in sheet form at points where a gasket must expand enough to allow air to accumulate, as with cover plates on supply tanks. Over a period of time, oil tends to deteriorate the material used in making neoprene gaskets. The condition of the gasket must, therefore, be checked whenever the unit is disassembled. Since neoprene gasket material is soft and flexible, it easily becomes misshapen, scratched or torn. Great care is, therefore, necessary in handling neoprene. Shellac, gasket sealing compounds or "pipe dope" should never be used with sheet neoprene, unless absolutely necessary for satisfactory installation.

28. Of the following, the one that is NOT mentioned in the above paragraph as a requirement for a good gasket material is that the material must be   28._____

    A. cheap
    B. unaffected by heat developed in a system
    C. relatively soft
    D. capable of maintaining required clearances

29. According to the above paragraph, neoprene will be affected by   29._____

    A. air   B. temperature
    C. pressure   D. oil

30. According to the above paragraph, care is necessary in handling neoprene because   30._____

    A. its condition must be checked frequently
    B. it tears easily
    C. pipe dope should not be used
    D. it is difficult to use

Questions 31-35.

DIRECTIONS: Questions 31 through 35, inclusive, should be answered in accordance with the following statements and instructions.

Column A below lists defects that often happen to equipment that is used in a sewage disposal plant. Column B shows the equipment that is used in such a plant. In the space at the right next to the number of the defect listed in Column A, select the letter in Column B representing the piece of equipment with which this defect is MOST closely associated.

COLUMN A	COLUMN B	
31. Broken shear pin	A. Centrifugal pump	31._____
32. Worn collector ring	B. Wound rotor motor	32._____
33. Pitted impeller	C. Bar screen	33._____
34. Worn chain	D. Methane-gas engine	34._____
35. Crankpin bearing		35._____

36. It is often said that in selecting a man for a job, dependability is more important than seniority. This is because

    A. it is difficult to judge the amount of work an older man can do
    B. an older man will know how to *avoid* work better
    C. the dependable man is the man you can count on to do the job as called for
    D. the dependable man will require fewer instructions

36.____

37. *A man may be conscientious, and yet not be efficient.* This statement MOST likely means that

    A. a man will not be able to do a job properly unless he has special training
    B. a man may want to do a job well, but may not know how to go about doing it
    C. if a man is efficient, he may not be conscientious
    D. the more conscientious a man is the less efficient he will be

37.____

38. If you were a senior sewage treatment worker, a good way of building up the morale of men assigned to you would be to

    A. overlook minor infractions of the rules
    B. pass the blame for bad assignments to your superiors
    C. treat the men fairly
    D. cover up for men who have made mistakes in their jobs

38.____

39. Threatening your subordinates with penalties for neglect of duty is

    A. *good* practice just to frighten them, even though the penalties will not be inflicted
    B. *poor* practice since men should never be threatened
    C. *good* practice if the penalty is actually going to be inflicted
    D. *poor* practice because men ought to work properly without threats

39.____

40. Of the following, the BEST indication that men are dissatisfied with their jobs is that they

    A. offer suggestions on improving operations
    B. appoint a grievance committee
    C. all join a union
    D. frequently leave for other jobs

40.____

41. If a senior sewage treatment worker must reprimand one of the men under him, the reprimand should be given

    A. in a loud tone of voice so that the man is properly impressed
    B. firmly but quietly
    C. the next day when the senior can get the man alone
    D. in front of the entire crew so that the rest of the men know what is right

41.____

42. If a senior sewage treatment worker is not sure of how a job should be done, he should

    A. make believe he does so that his men will not discover his lack of knowledge
    B. get someone else to do the job
    C. ask his superior how the job should be done
    D. put the job off until he can learn from another crew how it should be done

42.____

43. A senior sewage treatment worker makes a mistake, and admits it to his men.   43.____
This practice is _____, because the men _____.

    A. *good;* will respect him more
    B. *poor;* will not trust his judgment anymore
    C. *good;* will then learn to check everything he does before wasting time doing jobs improperly
    D. *poor;* should not know why a job is being done in the way it is

44. A supervisor can BEST earn the respect of his men by   44.____

    A. never criticizing his men
    B. taking the blame for all actions of his men
    C. defending his men from all criticism, regardless of whether the criticism is deserved or not
    D. defending his men from unsupported criticism

45. As a senior sewage treatment worker, you have been ordered by the engineer to do a job   45.____
in a certain manner which you think is not a good way of doing the job. You should

    A. tell the engineer you should be permitted to do the job in whatever way you feel best
    B. avoid doing the job
    C. do the job, but tell your men that you are not responsible for the method being used
    D. explain your objections to the engineer, but then do the job in whatever manner the engineer decides

46. The MOST important requirement for a good supervisor is to have   46.____

    A. physical strength   B. the ability to handle men
    C. manual dexterity   D. good appearance

47. A good senior sewage treatment worker should   47.____

    A. give all the disagreeable assignments to the laziest worker
    B. give all the good assignments to the best worker
    C. give disagreeable assignments to those men who have special training for them
    D. rotate disagreeable assignments among the men

48. A new sewage treatment worker has been assigned to work under you as a senior.   48.____
The MOST important information you should get from the new man is

    A. his age
    B. the type of work he likes to do
    C. his previous experience
    D. how well he gets along with other men

49. A member of your crew, who frequently comes to you with unjustified complaints, comes   49.____
to you again with another complaint.
You should

    A. cut the man short and tell him to stop complaining unnecessarily
    B. listen to the complaint, but do nothing about it
    C. listen to the complaint, and then tell the man the complaint is not justified
    D. check the complaint to see if it is justified

50. To insure that the men working under him are doing their work properly, a senior sewage   50.____
    treatment worker should

    A. check their work frequently
    B. have the men prepare a written report about the work
    C. assign one individual to be responsible for each job
    D. keep a record of the supplies they use

_____

KEY (CORRECT ANSWERS)

1. C	11. D	21. B	31. C	41. B
2. B	12. C	22. A	32. B	42. C
3. C	13. B	23. A	33. A	43. A
4. B	14. C	24. B	34. C	44. D
5. B	15. B	25. A	35. D	45. D
6. D	16. B	26. C	36. C	46. B
7. A	17. D	27. B	37. B	47. D
8. C	18. A	28. A	38. C	48. C
9. D	19. B	29. D	39. C	49. D
10. C	20. D	30. B	40. D	50. A

_____

BASIC FUNDAMENTALS
OF HYDRAULICS AND ELECTRICITY

TABLE OF CONTENTS

	Page
INTRODUCTION	1
HYDRAULICS	1
HYDRAULIC RADIUS	5
ELECTRICITY	18

BASIC FUNDAMENTALS OF
HYDRAULICS AND ELECTRICITY

There are similarities between fluids and electricity which help us to understand the fundamental of both. For example, we have the following units of measurement:

	Fluid	*Electricity*
Pressure	pounds per square inch (psi) or feet of water	electromotive force (emf) E or volts
Flow	gallons per minute (gpm) or cubic feet per second (cfs)	amperes (amp)
Resistance to flow	head loss feet of fluid or psi	resistance (ohms)
Quantity	gallons or cubic feet (gal) or (cf)	kilowatt hours (KWH)

Hydraulics

This is the name given to that branch of science which deals with fluids at rest and in motion. The former is sometimes spoken of as hydrostatics and the latter as hydrodynamics. We are concerned here mainly with water at rest and in motion. Many of the same principles apply to air and gases.

Consideration will be given to water moving or flowing through pipes, channels and pumps and ways of measuring the quantity flowing in a given time. We must be careful of units, the basic ones being:

Length in feet	ft
Area in square feet	sq ft or ft^2
Rate: gallons per minute	gpm.
million gallons per day	mgd
cu ft per second	cfs or sec ft
Weight: 1 gallon of water	8.34 lb
1 cu ft water	62.4 lb
Speed or velocity of flow in feet per second	ft/sec

Head. The precise meaning of the term *head* is the amount of energy possessed by a unit quantity of water at its given location. Ordinarily, the energy is expressed in *foot-pounds,* and the unit quantity of water considered is one pound. The head, then, is expressed in foot-pounds of energy per pound of water, or,

$$\frac{ft \times lb}{lb} = ft$$

Thus, all heads can be expressed in feet. Water may contain energy due to (a) its elevation, (b) its pressure, or (c) its velocity. These energies are called elevation (or static) head, pressure head, and velocity head, respectively. In addition, operators often have occasion to refer to *pump head,* which is the energy required for a pump to move one pound of water, and to *friction head,* which is the energy lost due to friction within the fluid and against the walls of the pipe or channel.

Elevation (or static) head. Elevations must be expressed as the vertical distance from some base level, or reference plane, such as mean sea level, the surface of the ground, or some other arbitrarily chosen level.
Then, for example, water that is 100 ft above the reference plane, has 100 ft-lbs of energy, and its elevation head is 100 ft.

Pressure head. Pressures are expressed in terms of force per unit area, such as pounds per square inch or pounds per square foot. One square foot contains 144 square inches. Therefore, a pressure of 1 lb/in^2 = 144 lb/ft^2, since every square inch is subjected to a force of one pound.
To calculate the energy per pound of water, we must consider the number of pounds of water in a unit volume, which is called the "density" of the water. The density of water is 62.4 lb/ft^3. Then if the pressure of the water is 1 lb/in^2 (often written 1 psi), the "pressure head" is

$$\frac{144 \; lb/ft^2}{62.4 \; lb/ft^3} = 2.3ft$$

or
1 psi = 2.3 ft pressure head

By the same kind of calculation, a water pressure of 40 psi equals

$$\frac{40 \times 144 \; lb/ft^2}{62.4 lb/ft^2} = 92.3 ft \text{ pressure head}$$

or
40 X 2.3 = 92.3 ft pressure head

Velocity head. The energy of motion is called kinetic energy, and is calculated by the relationship

$$Energy = \frac{mv^2}{2g}$$

where m represents the mass of the moving object, v its velocity, and g the force which gravity exerts on a mass of one pound.

In everyday speech, we are accustomed to expressing both force and mass in pounds. However, this causes confusion when energy calculations are attempted, because the force exerted by gravity is not numerically equal to the mass in pounds. That is to say, force and mass cannot properly be expressed in the same units.

One way of avoiding this difficulty is to speak of the force of gravity in terms of the acceleration it produces when it acts upon a unit mass. One of the fundamental laws of physics is that force equals mass times acceleration. Thus, the force on a unit mass of one pound is numerically equal to the acceleration.

Acceleration is the rate at which velocity changes. If an automobile goes from zero miles per hour to sixty miles per hour in two minutes, we can say that its average change of speed was thirty miles per hour in each minute, or thirty miles per hour per minute. Likewise, if water moving ten feet per second speeds up to fifteen feet per second, and the time required for the change of speed is one second, we could say that it accelerated five feet per second per second. Accelerations are often expressed in feet per second. The units can then be written ft/ sec. This is equivalent to writing $\dfrac{ft}{sec \times sec}$ or $\dfrac{ft}{sec^2}$

When gravity acts upon a free-falling body, it produces an acceleration of 32.2 ft/sec^2. This value of g can be used in the equation for calculating velocity head. If we consider, for example one pound of water moving with a velocity of 10 ft/sec, its velocity head is calculated as follows:

$$Energy = \frac{1\ lb \times 10\ ft\ /\ sec \times 10\ ft\ /\ sec}{2 \times 32.2\ ft\ /\ sec^2} = 1.5\ ft\text{-}lb$$

$$Velocity\ head = \frac{1.5\ ft\text{-}lb}{1\ lb} = 1.5\ ft$$

In the first of these two equations we multiplied by the weight of the water. In the second we divided by the weight of the water. Since these two operations cancel each other, the velocity head can be calculated by leaving out the weight in the first place:

$$Velocity\ head = \frac{v^2}{2g}$$

Friction head. Friction head equals the loss of energy due to friction within the liquid and friction against the walls of the pipe or channel. When we are dealing with water, the friction within the liquid is relatively small, and most of the energy is lost due to friction against the walls. Therefore, the friction loss depends mostly upon the characteristics of the material of which the pipe or channel is made and its surface smoothness. The usual procedure for estimating friction head losses is to use a table in an engineering handbook which gives directly the friction loss per foot of a particular kind of pipe or channel.

Pump head. The pump head equals the ft-lb of energy given to each pound of water passing through the pump.

Pumping. Pumps are used to move liquids to a higher level or to increase the rate of flow. Figure (1) and Figure (2) show two typical pumping conditions. To understand these figures it is necessary to know that in a liquid at rest the pressure at any point is equal to the weight of the liquid above the point, plus the weight of the atmosphere above the surface of the liquid. Both, must be expressed in the same units.

FIG. 1   FIG. 2

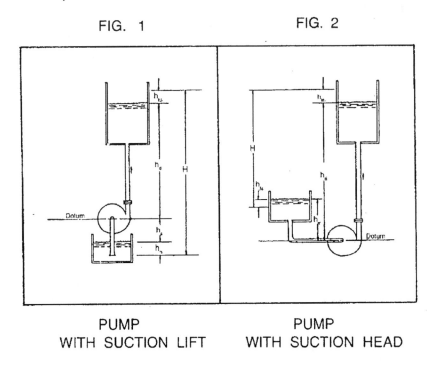

PUMP
WITH SUCTION LIFT

PUMP
WITH SUCTION HEAD

These units are usually pounds per square inch (psi) or feet of water. Since most pumping problems involve difference in pressure, the atmospheric pressure may be neglected and gauge pressures (psig) or height in feet may be used. Total head in feet at a point can be expressed as the height of a column of water whose weight would produce a certain pressure at that point. Psi X 2.31 = head in feet.

FIG. 3

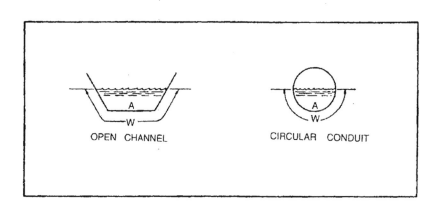

OPEN CHANNEL   CIRCULAR CONDUIT

HYDRAULIC RADIUS

For Figure 1— Pump operating with a suction lift:

$$H = h_d + h_s + h_{fd} + h_{fa} + \frac{V^2_d}{2g} \quad \frac{V^2_s}{2g}$$

For Figure 2 — Pump operating with suction head:

$$H = h_d + h_s + h_{fd} + h_{fa} + \frac{V^2_d}{2g} \quad \frac{V^2_s}{2g}$$

Where —

H = Total head in feet (formerly called total dynamic head) at which the pump operates.

h_d = Static discharge head in feet, or the vertical distance between the pump datum and liquid surface in the receiving tank. The pump datum is at the center line for horizontal pumps and at the entrance eye of the impeller for vertical pumps.

$h.$ = Static suction head or lift in feet or vertical distance between pump datum and liquid surface in the suction well.

h_{fd} = Friction head in discharge in feet or the head necessary to overcome friction in valves, fittings, etc. in the discharge piping.

h_{fs} = Friction head in suction in feet

g = 32.2 ft/sec^2 = Acceleration due to gravity.

$\frac{V^2_d}{2g}$ and $\frac{V^2_s}{2g}$ discharge nozzle and suction nozzle of the pump. When the nozzles are of the same diameter these values are equal and cancel out. Velocity head represents energy which the pump must deliver to the liquid but which is not measured by a pressure gage. It is the head required to give to the liquid the velocity "V" in feet per second.

The relationship between the volume of water flowing per unit of time, the velocity of the moving water and the size of pipe or channel through which the flow takes place may be expressed by the equation:

$$Q = AV$$

Where

Q = rate of flow or volume per unit time (usually expressed as cubic ft/sec (cfs)

A = Area through which water is flowing, measured at right angles in the direction of flow (usually expressed in sq ft)

V = Average velocity of flow or distance traveled per unit of time (usually expressed as ft/sec)

There are three general types of problems using the equation $Q = AV$. These are as follows:

1. The water in an open channel has been observed to flow a distance of 180 feet in 2 minutes. The dimensions of the channel are 2 feet wide and 18 inches deep. Compute the rate of flow

$$V = \frac{180}{2 \text{ min}} = \frac{90 \text{ ft}}{\text{min}} = \frac{1.5 \text{ ft}}{\text{sec}}$$

$$A = 2 \text{ ft} \times 18 \text{ in} \times \frac{\text{ft}}{12 \text{ in}} = 3.0 \text{ sq ft}$$

then

$$Q = AV = 3.0 \text{ sq ft} \times \frac{1.5 \text{ ft}}{\text{sec}} = 4.5 \text{ cfs}$$

2. A meter shows water flowing through a 12 inch diameter pipe at the rate of 2 mgd. To determine the velocity of the water

$$Q = \frac{2,000,000 \text{ gal}}{\text{day}} \times \frac{\text{cu ft}}{7.5 \text{ gal}} \times \frac{\text{day}}{24 \text{ hr}} \times \frac{\text{hr}}{60 \text{ min}} \times \frac{\text{min}}{60 \text{ sec}} = 3.08 \text{ cfs}$$

$$A = \pi r^2 = 3.1416 \times 6 \text{ in} \times 6 \text{ in} \times \frac{\text{sq ft}}{144 \text{ sq ft}} = 0.79 \text{ sq ft}$$

then $$V = Q / A = \frac{3.08 \text{ cu ft}}{0.79 \text{ sq ft} \times \text{sec}} = 3.9 \frac{\text{ft}}{\text{sec}}$$

3. Baffles are to be placed in a coagulation tank so that the velocity of flow between baffles is 0.3 ft/sec. The depth of flow in the tank is 8 feet and the rate of flow through the tank is 2 mgd. Find the distance, w between baffles.

$$Q = 2 \text{mgd} \times 1.55 \frac{\text{cfs}}{\text{mgd}} = 3.08 \text{ cfs}$$

V=0.3 ft/sec
let the distance between baffles equal w

$$\text{then } A = 8 \times w = \frac{Q}{V} = 3.08 \frac{\text{cu ft}}{\text{sec}} \times \frac{\text{sec}}{0.3 \text{ ft}}$$

$$W = \frac{3.08 \text{ cu ft / sec}}{8 \text{ ft} \times 0.3 \text{ ft / sec}} = 1.28 \text{ ft}$$

Pipe Friction. The h_{fd} and h_{fs}. in the preceding paragraphs are those portions of the total head necessary to overcome friction between the fluid and the walls of the suction and discharge piping. The values of these terms depend upon the length of the pipeline, its diameter, the velocity of the flowing liquid and the condition of the internal walls of the pipe, usually called the roughness factor. These influences are expressed in the formula

$$h_f = \text{Friction head} = f\frac{L}{d}\frac{V^2}{2g}$$

Where f = roughness factor
       L = length of pipe
       d = diameter

$$\frac{V^2}{2g} = \text{velocity head}$$

Tables are available for the value of f, which varies with both V and d in this formula. The value of f is fractional, varying from .04 for small V and d to .01 for large values of V and d. Another formula derived from this basic one expresses the roughness factor as a whole number known as the C value in the Hazen & Williams formula. Tables and a special slide rule have been developed for solving pipe problems by this formula. The value of C varies from 140 for very smooth large pipe to a low of 40 or less for badly corroded or dirty pipe. See Figure 4 (Flow Chart for value "C" equals 100)

FIG. 4

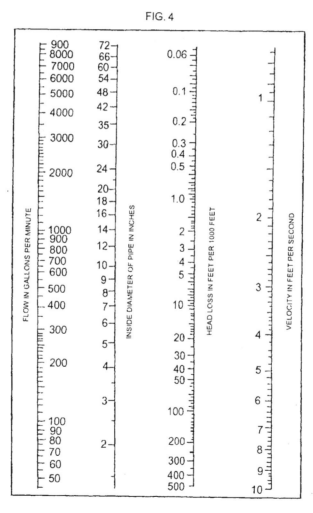

FLOW CHART
"C" 100
Based on the Hazen-Williams Formula

FIG. 5

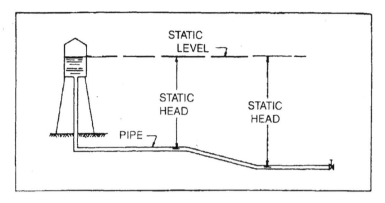

STATIC HEAD

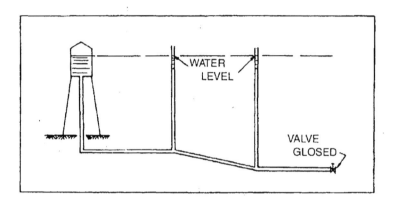

WATER LEVEL, NO FLOW IN PIPE

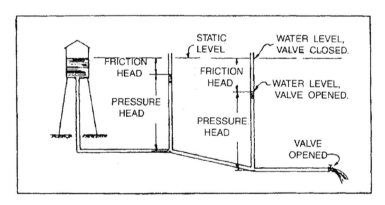

PRESSURE HEAD

If vertical open pipes are attached in a pipe line as shown in Figure 6, the water level in the pipes will stand at a level even with the elevation of the water in the storage tank. If the outlet valve is opened to permit water to flow, the level of the water in the vertical pipes will drop. The drop in the level or loss in head is the "friction head" and represents the energy lost by friction of the water flowing through the pipe.

Power Requirements for Pumping. Work must be done to move liquid against the total heads (H) indicated in Figures 8 and 9. The unit of work is the foot pound which is the amount of work or energy required to lift one pound a vertical distance of one foot. The common unit of power or rate of doing work is horsepower (hp). One horsepower is equal to 33,000 ft. lbs. per minute. In electrical units, one horsepower is equivalent to 746 watts.

The power required to drive a pump can be computed as follows:
Work done by the pump (or water horsepower) = Whp

$$Whp = \frac{lbs.\,of\,water\,raised\,per\,minute\,X\,H}{33,000}$$

$$= \frac{gpm\,X\,8.34\,X\,H}{33,000} = \frac{gpm\,X\,H}{3,960}$$

Example: The sum of the elevation, pressure, velocity and friction heads is 100 ft. What would be the work done by the pump or the horsepower required (water horsepower) if 50 gallons per minute is pumped?

$$Whp = \frac{gal\,/\,min\,X\,lbs\,/\,gal\,X\,ft\,lbs\,/\,lb}{ft\text{-}lbs\,/\,min}$$

=1.26 horsepower

Since all the power delivered by the driving unit cannot be converted to useful work, the ratio between output and input is called pump efficiency.
Power required to drive the pump, or "brake horsepower" is computed by this formula:

$$bhp = \frac{whp}{pump\,eff} = \frac{gpm\,X\,8.33\,X\,H}{33,000\,X\,pump\,eff} = \frac{gpm\,X\,H}{3960\,X\,pump\,eff}$$

If the efficiency (eff) of the pump is 65%

$$\frac{1.26}{0.65} = 1.94 \text{ horsepower must be delivered to the pump.}$$

Again since motors are not 100% efficient

$$Motor\,hp = \frac{whp}{pump\,eff\,X\,motor\,eff}$$

$$= \frac{gpm\,X\,H}{3960\,X\,pump\,eff\,X\,motor\,eff}$$

If the motor efficiency is 80%

$$\frac{1.26}{0.65\,X\,0.80} = 2.425$$

horsepower must be delivered to the motor in order to pump 50 gpm against a total head of 100 feet.

Flow in Open Channels. Flow in open conduits and in partially filled pipes is affected by the same factors as in pipes flowing full. These factors determine the slope required for an open channel to maintain a certain flow and velocity. The velocity, is actually determined by the slope of the water surface, but this is usually also the slope of the bottom of the channel and the water flows at a constant depth. The slope of the water surface is called the hydraulic gradient. The friction between water and the conduit walls depends upon the roughness of the surface, but the formula for it is different because the liquid now has a free surface and the length of contact depends upon the shape of the channel and the depth of flow. These factors are combined in the " hydraulic radius," which is found by dividing the cross-sectional area of the flowing water by the distance around that area along the walls of the channel. This distance is called the "wetted perimeter" of the channel (see Figure 3). Thus,

$$\text{Hyd Rad } r = \frac{A}{W} \text{feet(figure3)}$$

From these considerations, there has been developed the Chezy formula:

$v = C\sqrt{rs}$ feet per sec

where C = coefficient based on roughness, slope and value of r.

s = slope of the hydraulic gradient or water surface in open channels, usually expressed as ft per foot or ft per thousand feet. Thus, a slope of .004 indicates a drop of four feet in a thousand foot length.

The two principal formulas for determining C, the Kutter and the Manning formulas, depend largely upon values of "n" which is the coefficient of friction. These values have become quite well known for various types of surfaces and materials. Thus n=.013 is commonly used for design of vitrified tile pipes and for large diameter pre-cast concrete pipes.

Tables and diagrams have been published from which velocities, rates of flow and slopes can be determined for various diameters of pipes and values of "n".

Weirs. There are numerous ways of measuring flowing water, but three devices most commonly used are weirs, Venturi meters, and Parshall flumes.

The weir consists of rectangular opening or V notch opening with sharp edges. The weir is set vertically so that the flow passes over it tnd falls away from it.

FIG. 6

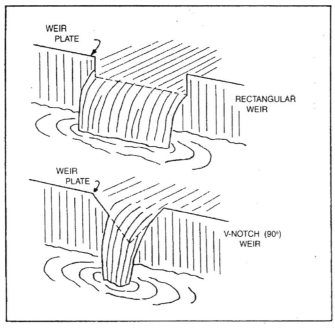

WEIRS

It is only necessary to measure the height of water above the crest of the weir at a point sufficiently upstream which avoids the curve of the water surface over the weir. In placing a weir, two points must be considered. First, the weir should be installed in the channel so that the velocity of the water approaching the weir is relatively low. Second, the "head" on the weir is not the depth of water as it passes over the weir proper but is the difference in elevation between the edge of the weir and the water upstream a short distance. In Figure 7 both of these points are illustrated. By using the head measurement the flow is determined from the formula:

Rate of flow $Q = 3.33 \, L \, h\sqrt{h}$ cfs (for a suppressed weir) and

$$Q = 3.33 \left(L - \frac{h}{5}\right) h. \, \sqrt{h} \text{ cfs (for a contracted weir)}$$

where h = the height of horizontal water surface above crest of weir, L= horizontal length of weir.

The V notch weir is more accurate than the rectangular weir for small flows. For a 90 degree notch, the formula is: (Figure 8)

$Q = Ch^2 \, \sqrt{h}$ cfs where

C is a coefficient depending upon the material of the weir and the range of head. Values of C are given in handbooks for various materials and heads. The V notch weir is suitable for measuring flows from 10 to 3,500 gpm.

Another formula which may be used with a V notch weir with

90° angle is

$Q = 2.5h^{5/2}$

where   Q   = rate of discharge in cfs

       h   = "head" on weir in feet (Figure 8)

Using the chart. (Figure 8)
    If h is measured to be 0.20 feet then Q = .045cfs
                                          = 21 gpm

FIG. 7

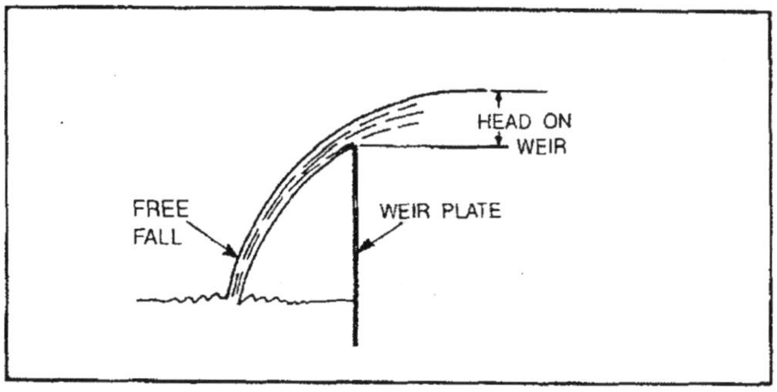

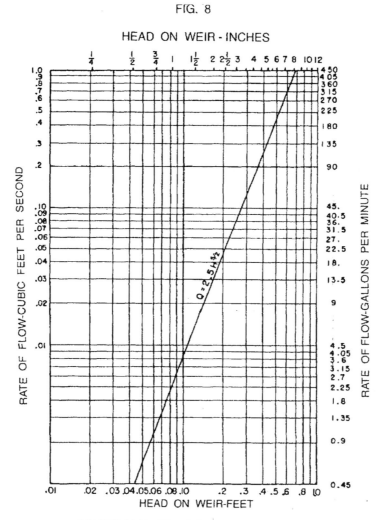

HEAD ON WEIR

FIG. 8

90° V-NOTCH WEIR FORMULA-Q=2.5H5/2

Venturi Meter. This type of flow measuring device is installed in a pipe line and consists of a throat carefully machined to a given inside diameter, a converging section which tapers from the pipe diameter to the throat and a diverging section from the throat to the pipe diameter. (See Figure 9) Taps are provided for measuring pressure head at points just before convergence and at the throat. The only measurement necessary to compute the flow is the difference in pressure head between the two tap points. Figure 10 shows graphically how pressure and velocity heads change in the Venturi Meter.

Parshall Flume. This type of flow measuring device was developed for measuring irrigation water in open channels where there may be debris and silt and where little loss of head can be permitted.

FIG. 9

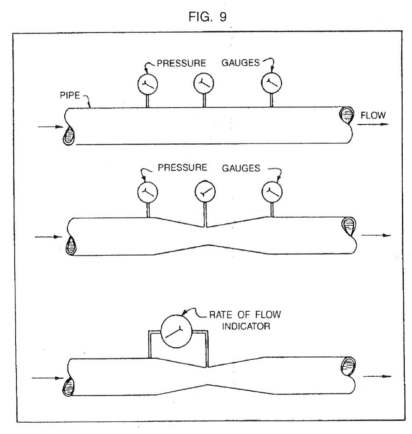

VENTURI TUBE

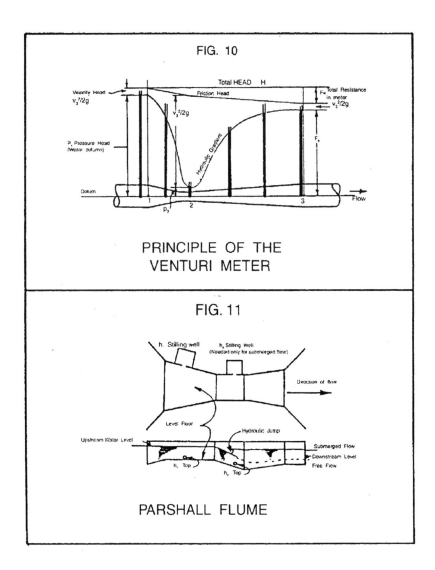

FIG. 10

PRINCIPLE OF THE
VENTURI METER

FIG. 11

PARSHALL FLUME

In principle, the flume is similar to the Venturi meter. It has an inlet section with sides converging slowly to a throat of fixed dimensions and an outlet section diverging more rapidly to the original channel width. For the usual non-submerged condition only measurement of the depth of water at a fixed distance upstream from the throat is necessary to determine the flow. The flume may be constructed of almost any building material. For greatest accuracy the throat is often made to accurate dimensions from corrosion resistant metal. Figure 11 illustrates the Parshall Flume.

Magnetic Flow Meter. Bach of the previously described flow measuring devices involves an appreciable loss of head. A new development consists of a non-magnetic tube of the same internal diameter as the pipe line across which a magnetic field is established. Water flowing through the magnetic field produces a voltage proportional to the velocity. This voltage is converted by electrical and mechnical means to indicate and record the rate of flow.

An important operating and maintenance requirement of any flow measuring device is that pressure connecting stilling wells, floats and float tubes must be kept clean.

Rate of Flow Controllers. These are used to maintain flows at constant rates. Generally, all of the newer models depend on the Venturi principle to control a movable diaphragm or a pilot valve. This in turn actuates a main valve so as to control the size of an opening so that the desired amount of water is passed. Figure 12 shows a section through one type of controller. Actually this particular type of controller has two valves on the vertical stem and two valve seats but, for simplification, only one has been shown.

FIG. 12

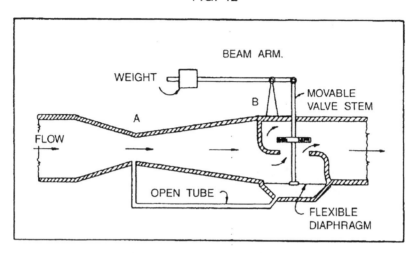

RATE OF FLOW CONTROLLER

The weight is placed at the desired point on the beam arm which corresponds to a certain rate of flow through the valve. At this particular rate of flow the unit pressure at point "A" will be less than the unit pressure at point "B". The unit pressure at point A is transferred, by means of the small open tube, to the compartment below the flexible diaphragm. The downward total pressure on the diaphragm is then greater than the upward total pressure. This results in a tendency for the valve stem to move downward. This tendency is counteracted by the weight at the proper location on the beam arm. At the desired rate of flow everything is in balance.

Pumps. Pumps have many uses in waterworks practice. Though there are many types, practically all water pumps may be classified into two general categories: displacement pumps and velocity pumps.

Displacement pumps employ some mechanical means (plungers, pistons, gears or cams) for forcing specific volumes of water through the units. Velocity pumps impart a high velocity to water and convert the velocity head into pressure head which forces the water through the apparatus.

Either type of pump raises the pressure on inlet side to a higher pressure on the outlet side. The specific means for bringing this about are quite different for the two types. Displacement type pumps, when operating at a particular speed, will take specific unit volumes of water and mechanically force the water out of the pump at a certain rate without regard to conditions beyond the pumping unit. When the resistance to flow beyond the pump is increased, the pressure will be increased. The only limit is the available horsepower and the physical strength of the discharge pipe or the pump. In other words, if something goes wrong on the discharge side of the pump to stop the flow, something may have to "give" and serious damage may result.

This is not the case with a velocity pump. A velocity pump merely causes the water to move with a very high velocity within the pump, usually in a circular direction. Under most conditions the amount of water which passes through the pump depends upon the resistance to flow on the discharge side. If the resistance is too great, for example if a valve is closed, the pump will continue to operate. This will produce the maximum pressure obtainable from that particular pump and speed of operation, but no wa.ter will pass through the pump. Probably no damage will result unless the pump is allowed to run until it over heats.

Displacement pumps may be subdivided into two general types-reciprocating and rotary. The reciprocating type, equipped with either plungers or pistons, includes direct acting, single or duplex, steam pumps, crank and flywheel pumps, and plunger pumps. Rotary pumps may be either cam, screw or gear types.

Velocity pumps may be subdivided into several general types including centrifugal, propeller, mixed flow, and turbine units.

Displacement pumps have certain advantages over velocity types. In displacement pumps the quantity of liquid delivered does not vary with the discharge head; they are easily primed; many act like air pumps and prime themselves when the suction head is low. They will operate smoothly on high suction lifts up to 25 feet or so. For high heads and small quantities the reciprocating pump is probably still the best. For many applications, the velocity pump, particularly the centrifugal pump, has displaced the reciprocating pump. Advantages of velocity pumps are lower initial cost, generally higher efficiency and easier installation and maintenance.

FIG. 13

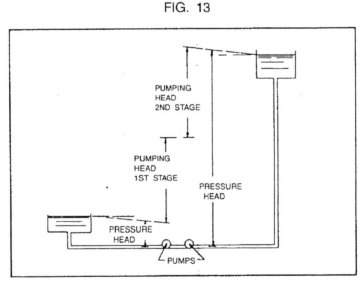

TWO STAGE PUMPING

Centrifugal Pumps. In the centrifugal pump, pressure is developed almost entirely by centrifugal force. Water enters at the center of an impeller which is rotated at high speed. Pressure is exerted and water moves to the outside. A specially shaped casing around the impeller discharges the water through a single opening to discharge line. There are various types of impellers. These include the open type which is commonly" used for pumping sewage and the closed type which is commonly used for pumping clear water. The water may enter at one side of the impeller in the side suction pump or on both sides in the double suction pump. Two or more pumps are used in stages when pumping against high heads. More than one stage can be obtained by using several impellers mounted on a single shaft. Also, two individual pumps can be mounted on a single shaft, driven by one motor, when the head conditions are high. The application of a multistage layout is illustrated in Figure 13.

Centrifugal pumps may be operated with'suction lifts. With all but minimum lifts, priming arrangements may be required.

The performance and operating characteristics are given on a pump curve sheet supplied by the manfacturer for each pump. On Figure 14 the curves show the discharge in gallons per minute (gpm) of the pump at various heads, the pump efficiency under different head-discharge conditions and the brake horsepower under various head-discharge conditions. As the head increases the discharge decreases until the shut-off head is reached.

FIG. 14

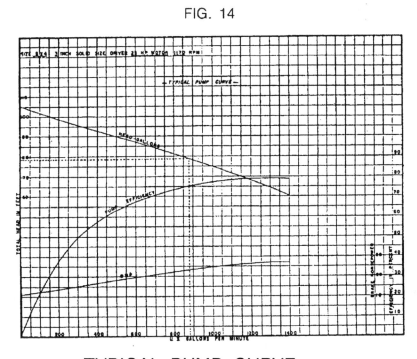

TYPICAL PUMP CURVE

On the pump curves, Figure 14, dotted lines indicate how values can be read from these curves. The pump for which these curves were prepared, when operated at 1170 revolutions per minute (rpm), will deliver 880 gpm at a total head of 79 feet. The brake horsepower (bhp) of the pump is 23 and the pump efficiency 75%. For a motor with an efficiency of 92 percent, the mhp (motor horsepower) should be 25. (Refer to power requirement for pumping). The shutoff head at which no water is delivered is 105 feet.

Large centrifugal pumps usually operate at slow speeds to minimize wear and maintenance costs.

The other velocity pumps have, in general, similar operating characteristics. They may vary considerably in construction and have different applications to water pumping problems. Propeller types are usually limited to low heads and the turbine type, with several stages, is most often used as a deep well pump.

Electricity

Electrical Units. The volt, as indicated in the introduction to this chapter, expresses electrical pressure just as feet, head or psi expresses water pressure. It is represented by the symbol "E", or sometimes emf, the abbreviation for electro-motive force.

For years, standard voltages have been 110, 220, 440, 2,200, 4,400 and 13,200. In water plants the voltage seldom exceeds 440. Higher voltages are used primarily for transmission lines. In some places the 110 and 220 standards have been replaced by 120 and 208. High voltages require proper equipment to prevent leaks (short circuits), and must be respected for personal-safety. Even pressures as low as 110 volts can be fatal.

Proper equipment should be used for the voltage furnished. If the average voltage is 120 on lighting circuits, then 120 and not 110 volt lamps should be used. They will last about three times as long.

For motors over 50 hp, voltages in excess of 440 is desirable. For 5 to 50 hp motors, economy dictates the use of 220 and 440 volts.

The ampere (amp) in electricity expresses the rate of flow, as gpm expresses water flows. In equations, the ampere is represented by I. Just as large pipes are required for large flows of water, large wire sizes are required for hea.vy amperages to keep down the losses due to resistance. Voltage drop due to resistance is similar to head loss due to friction in a pipe line.

Every electrical device has a current rating depending upon its design and resistance to flow. In motors the current varies with the load. Wires, fuses and switches are rated as to the current which they may safely carry. These ratings are fixed by a National Electric Code and should not be exceeded. An appliance rated for 25 amps should be protected by a fuse of that capacity to act as a safety valve. When carrying more than their rated capacity, wires and appliances overheat and may burn out or cause fires.

The ohm is the unit of electrical resistance. In electrical circ-cuits the loss of voltage, voltage drop, or loss in pressure is proportional to the resistance and the rate of current flow. Thus we have the simple relation known as Ohm's Law: $E = RI$. Values of resistance R for unit lengths or conductors of various sizes and materials are found in handbooks.

Direct and Alternating Currents. If the current flows first in one and then the other direction, it is known as alternating current and the number of times per second that it flows in each direction determines the number of cycles. A current that flows in any one direction 60 times per second is called 60 cycle. This is the standard for alternating current in this country.

Transformers are used to increase or decrease voltage. They consist of two stationary coils of wire insulated from each other but wound around a common iron core. Current flowing through the primary coil induces a current in the secondary with a voltage related to the number of turns of wire on the primary and secondary coils.

The Watt (W) is the unit of electrical power (P) and is most commonly used as a thousand watts or the kilowatt (KW). The mechanical unit of power or horsepower (HP) is equivalent to 746 watts. For rough computation it can be remembered that horsepower is approximately equivalent to three-quarters of a KW. Since the efficiency of many small motors is about 75%, one kilowatt in-put is roughly equivalent to one HP out-put.

For direct current:

$P = E\,I$. By substitution for E,

$P = R\,I^2$, or by substitution for I

$$P = \frac{E^2}{R}$$

From these expressions it can be seen that power varies directly with both current and voltage if resistance is not considered, but as the square of either one when resistance is considered.

The "kilowatt hour" is the unit of cost for electricity. As the term indicates, it is the average power requirement in KW multiplied by the time in hours over which it is used.

The "single phase circuit" or two-wire system shown in Figure 15 is the simplest circuit. Figure 15 shows a single phase, three-wire system that can furnish two voltages. The three phase (three-wire) is the standard system for large motors. There are two different arrangements of leads from generators or transformers known as delta, Figure 16 and Y shown in Figure 16. Lighting circuits can be taken off as shown. However, unless motors are small, it is better to separate power and lighting circuits to avoid dimming of the lights when motors start.

Circuit protection is provided by fuses enclosed in some type of flame-proof case. They are not always suitable and more complicated thermal relays, air circuit breakers or oil breakers, are required to allow a heavy flow of current for a short time before acting. To allow for a heavy flow, these devices are needed with large motors. A special oil is used in circuit breakers. No other should be used. When a circuit breaker operates frequently, cause should be investigated and corrective steps taken. Protective devices should never be "jumped."

Grounding is extremely important and must be maintained.

Most alternating current "motors" are either of the induction or synchronous type. Synchronous motor speed is determined by the formula,

N =120 F/P when
N = revolutions of motor per minute (rpm)
F = frequency, cycles per second
P = number of poles
For 60 cycles, N = 7200/P

Thus, the fewer the poles, the faster the speed and the smallest possible number of poles is two. Since there must be an even number of poles, the greatest synchronous speed possible for 60 cycles is 3,600 r.p.m. Other possible speeds are 1,800 r.p.m., 1,200 r.p.m., 900 r.p.m., 450 r.p.m. and so forth. The synchronous motor operates accurately at the given speed. This is valuable for clocks and timing devices. However, the synchronous motor has definite poles which must be excited or magnetized by some source of direct current. Synchronous motors have low starting torque (or power), which makes them unsatisfactory for many loads. For this reason it is fortunate that centrifugal pumps can usually be started with small load. Synchronous motors are sometimes used because of their favorable power factor on extremely large pumps.

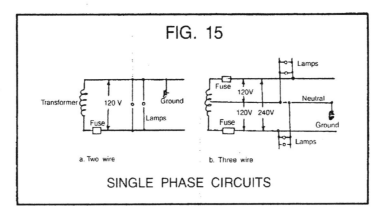

ELECTRIC CIRCUITS

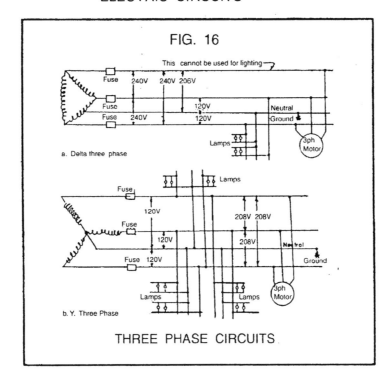

Induction motors. These motors have no poles which need excitation, and can be operated at variable speeds. They are sometimes called squirrel cage motors, because the rotor is made up of bars parallel to the shaft. Without a load, this type of motor will run at a speed close to the synchronous speed. As the load increases, the speed is reduced until at full load the speed is from 2% to 4% less than the synchronous speed. If the load is sufficiently increased, the motor will stop, or "pull out".

Induction motors require relatively small starting currents. Maintenance calls for keeping air ducts and windings of the motor clean. Oil in bearings should be flushed and changed at least once per year. The smaller motors require no special starting devices, and may be started directly across the line. Larger motors usually require reduced voltage for starting.

Variable speed is obtained in an induction motor by having a wound rotor, in whose circuit an external resistance may be added.

Thus a manufacturer can build a motor with external controls to give any speed and power which is required.

"Motor ratings", as well as the ratings for other electrical equipment, are based upon the temperature rise which will occur during operation continuously at normal full load and proper voltage. This rise is usually limited to 40 or 45 degrees centigrade. Thus, a motor may run hot to the touch and still be within its safe rating. A thermometer should be used to check the temperature on small motors. Large motors usually have temperature measuring devices built into them.

———

PUMPS

TABLE OF CONTENTS

	Page
Reciprocating Pumps	1
Maintenance of Reciprocating Pumps	1
Adjustment of Stroke	1
Pump Alignment	3
Scored Water Cylinder	4
Scored Steam Cylinder	4
Overhauling Water End Valves	4
Operation of Reciprocating Pumps	5
Failure to Start	5
Failure to Take Suction	6
Loss of Discharge Pressure	6
Centrifugal Pumps	7
Operation of Centrifugal Pumps	7
Starting a Centrifugal Pump	7
Operating a Centrifugal Pump	8
Securing a Centrifugal Pump	9
Maintenance of Centrifugal Pumps	9
Inspection and Renewal of Wearing Rings	9
Bearing Maintenance	11
Lubricating Systems	12
Replacing Pump Rotors	13
Pump Control Devices	17
Safety Precautions for Operating Pumps	18

PUMPS

This chapter contains information on the inspection and repair of reciprocating and centrifugal pumps and on the operation and repair of pressure regulating and speed limiting governors.

RECIPROCATING PUMPS

Reciprocating pumps were formerly the most widely used type of pump installed. At present, centrifugal and rotary pumps are far more common. Reciprocating pumps are used for two purposes _____ as fire and bilge pumps, and as emergency feed pumps.

MAINTENANCE OF RECIPROCATING PUMPS

When repairs are undertaken, a repair guide list should be used to make sure that every part of the pump which required attention or contributed to poor performance is put into proper condition. When a partial overhaul is undertaken, check "NOT DONE" for items that are not repaired. This will show that every part was inspected and either worked on or not worked on. Upon completion of a pump overhaul, the repair guide list can be kept as a permanent record of all measurements taken and all work done.

When a pump is disassembled for repair or inspection, all applicable blueprints and the manufacturer's technical manuals should be on hand. Micrometer measurements should be taken of the steam and water cylinders and the steam valve chest; these measurements are made on the fore and aft and athwartship diameters at the top, middle, and bottom. The results should be recorded in the Material History, with a sketch showing measurements taken.

The following paragraphs contain information on repair procedures for steam-driven reciprocating pumps.

Adjustment Of Stroke

In order for a steam-driven reciprocating pump to operate properly, the steam piston must travel a little beyond counterbore (fig. 4-1); this means that the pump must operate with a full stroke. A full stroke will result in more even wear throughout the cylinder.

When a pump does not have full stroke, the steam piston travel must be adjusted. A short stroke results in incomplete cushioning and the formation of shoulders in the steam cylinder, which may result in breakage of the piston rings. These shoulders will have to be removed before full stroke can be obtained. A stroke that is too long is usually indicated by a heavy metallic knock in the steam cylinder. Pumps should not be operated when the stroke is too long or too short.

The length of the stroke is adjusted by moving the two adjustable tappet collars on the threaded portion of the valve rod link. The tappet moves between the tappet collars as the lever is moved by the action of the piston rod.

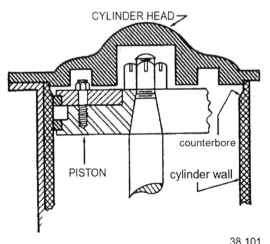

38.101

Figure 4-1. - Steam piston at upper end of stroke.

To shorten the stroke of the pump, turn the tappet collar in the direction that moves it toward the tappet. To lengthen the stroke of the pump, turn the tappet collar in the direction that moves it away from the tappet. Once the tappet collars have been set properly, they should be left alone. If it becomes necessary to adjust the tappet collars frequently while the pump is operating, the pump should be stopped and disassembled as soon as possible. The trouble may be in the operating linkage, the auxiliary piston valve, or the main piston valve.

Properly adjusted tappet collars will ensure a full stroke for the various pump loads and speeds. Refer to manufacturer's drawings and technical manuals for detailed information as to the method to be followed for specific types of valve gear. The following method may be used for a general guide if the appropriate information is not available. Place the steam piston and auxiliary piston valve on the center or half stroke. Then move each tappet collar so that it will be one-half the width of the steam port away from the tappet. Next start the pump. If the stroke is too short, move the tappet collars further apart. If the stroke is too long, move the tappet collars closer together. Make certain that the tappets are moved an equal amount, or the stroke will be longer on one end than on the other. When final adjustment has been made, lock the tappet collars securely in place.

Run the pump slowly, with the throttle cracked, against little or no pressure, and with the cushioning valves wide open. The piston should be striking on the cylinder heads (if it does not, there is friction at some point). Close down on the cushioning valves until the pump is running at full stroke and with smooth reversal and no striking. If it is impossible to obtain smoothness of reversal, it may be necessary to adjust the tappet collars.

In figure 4-2 the steam piston and pilot valves are shown beginning the up stroke. Both valves are in the upper position, thereby admitting high pressure steam through the lower steam inlet port to the underside of the steam piston, and permitting steam above the piston to escape through the exhaust port.

When the steam piston reaches the top of the stroke the lever and tappet linkage move the pilot (auxiliary piston valve) down, opening port A to the annular exhaust space above the center of the auxiliary and main piston valve. See figure 4-2. Opening port A releases pressure in space B, below the main piston valve, and permits the unbalanced higher pressure in space C to force the main piston valve down. The small size of the equalizing port in the main piston valve prevents the escape of any appreciable amount of high pressure steam into space B. The pilot valve blanks off the upper port, preventing the escape of high pressure steam from space C, even after the downward movement of the main piston valve uncovers port C, and thereby ensures complete movement of the piston valve to its lower position.

At the end of its travel, the main piston valve cushions itself when it blanks off the port to space A, trapping dead steam which cannot readily escape through the small equalizing port in the valve. The initial condition of steam balance is reestablished by means of this equalizing port. The previously described movements are repeated on the opposite end of the stroke.

The force which actuates the main piston valve is determined by the difference in the rate of flow of steam through port A, which is 1/4 inch in diameter, and through the 1/16-inch equalizing port drilled through the outside collars of the main piston valve. Except when the main piston valve is actually in motion, it is in complete balance, both axially and circumferentially, so that the friction between the sliding surfaces is the only force restricting its travel. The equalizing port, which connects the outer ends of the auxiliary piston valve cylinder, is essential to permit free movement of the auxiliary piston valve. Light packing will suffice for the valve actuating rod, since

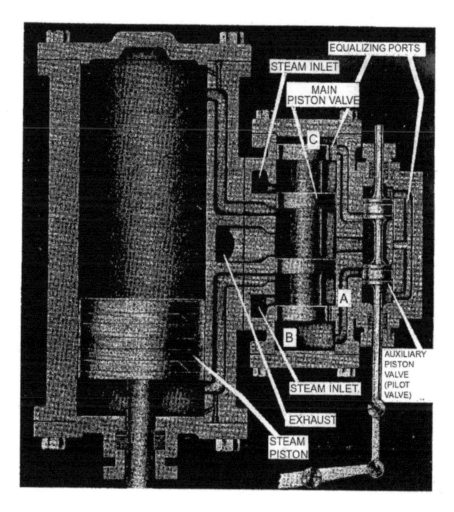

Figure 4-2. -Steam and assembly for a reciprocating pump.

38.99X

only auxiliary exhaust pressures must be held.

Pump Alignment

Improper alignment is one of the most frequent sources of trouble with pumps. Pumps with mountings secured to a bulkhead are more subject to misalignment than those with independent bases. A pump may have been properly aligned in the shop and then pulled out of line when bolted to the bulkhead mounting; or after the pump mounting was secured, the ship may have changed shape sufficiently to warp the bulkhead and cause misalignment.

Operation of an improperly aligned pump usually scores the rod and cylinders, and breaks the followers. The alignment of pumps should be tested occasionally by removing the piston and plunger and running a line through the steam and water cylinders. This should be performed as a routine test within the first year after a ship is commissioned; and also for a pump that is scoring rods or cylinders, or breaking followers.

Before a line is run through the cylinder or any adjustments are made, the foundation must be lined up and the centerline must be determined. The centerline must divide each cylinder equally (see fig. 4-3). Fasten one end of the line to a temporary beam at the end of one of the cylinders. In figure 4-3 the beam is rigged above the steam cylinder. Run the line down the center of both cylinders, and center it at the top and bottom of the steam cylinder, so that it

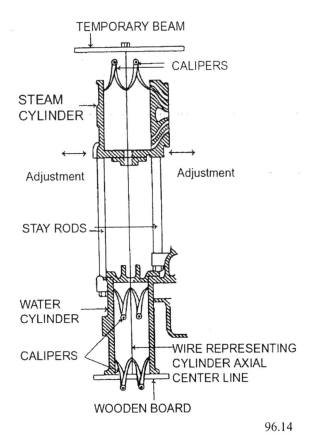

TEMPORARY BEAM

CALIPERS

STEAM CYLINDER

Adjustment   Adjustment

STAY RODS

WATER CYLINDER

CALIPERS

WIRE REPRESENTING CYLINDER AXIAL CENTER LINE

WOODEN BOARD

96.14

Figure 4-3. -Centering a line through two cylinders

becomes the axis of that cylinder. Then align the water cylinder with the steam cylinder. If realignment is necessary, the water cylinder may be moved and centered on the line without affecting the centering of the line on the steam cylinder.

To make a rough check of alignment of a pump, pull the steam and liquid end rod packing and check the clearances between the piston rods and the cylinder throat bushings. Make this check with the pistons in each of three positions-top, center, and bottom of the stroke. If clearance is not uniform, but the throat bushings are not worn out of round, realign the pump as soon as possible.

In some cases, when steam cylinder foundation pad bolts are slacked off, the cylinder pads pull away from the foundation as much as 1/2 inch, indicating settling of foundations and bulkheads. Correct this by fitting shims between the foundation and the pump.

A frequent cause of misalignment is the piping. The piping should line up naturally with the pump connections and should not be forced into position. Provision must be made in steam and exhaust lines to allow for expansion. All piping should be supported independently of the pump. Improperly installed piping puts a strain on the pump and forces it out of alignment. Special care should be taken to avoid vapor pockets when installing suction piping.

Scored Water Cylinder

When a water cylinder becomes scored, it is not always necessary to rebore the cylinder or renew the liner. Slight leakage from wear can usually be corrected by stoning the cylinder liner and renewing the packing. If reboring must be done, consult the tolerances allowed inboring cylinders, given in chapter 40 of BuShips Technical Manual. Reboring or renewal of the liner should be considered only when the scoring is extensive and rapid wearing of the packing takes place.

Scored Steam Cylinder

Scoring in a steam cylinder, even though of a minor nature, necessitates reboring to prevent steam leakage past the piston. The presence of such leakage is indicated by a dullness and discoloration of the cylinder walls. Once leakage has started, steam will gradually cut away cylinder walls until piston leakage becomes so excessive as to interfere with proper operation of the pump.

Overhauling Water End Valves

All valves in the water end of the pump must be kept tight to ensure satisfactory and economical pump operation. Valves may be faced in a lathe and then ground in on their seats by a simple device which consists of a length of rod slotted to fit a piece of metal which seats across the top of the valve.

It is sometimes desirable to take a cut off the valve seat without removing it. A simple cutter can be made with an extension for a bit-stock, similar to the grinding-in device. When flat valves are fitted, the seats may be trued up by using a small surface plate and spotting-in the section on the surface plate.

After the valves have been ground in, test the valves by closing the suction valve, opening the discharge valve, starting the pump, and noting the vacuum that the pump is capable of attaining.

At each examination, check all metal valve disks with a straightedge to see if they are true. The life of rubber valves can be lengthened by trimming and turning the valve sand by inserting brass backings.

Tension on the valve springs should be great enough to ensure a quick closing of the valve, but not so great that the valve cannot be lifted easily by hand. See that the springs are well secured by split pins, and adjust the valves to give the proper lift. Lift should be such that the circumferential opening is slightly greater than the clear opening through the seat, but NOT greater than 1/4 the diameter of the clear opening.

Keep the valves clean. A light mineral oil makes a good cleaner, and a lye or soda solution is satisfactory for removing caked or gummed oil from the valves.

In pumps having valve seats secured only by a taper fit, the seats should be forced home by a jack resting on the end of a reseater which in turn rests on the face of the valve seat. If the seat works loose, peen the edge of the seat slightly. In pumps that have the valve seats screwed into the pump diaphragm, always insert the valve seats with white lead; otherwise it will be difficult to remove them.

In some pumps, discharge valve seats in the water end are secured to the pump diaphragm by shoulders on the valve stems, where the stems screw into the suction seats. These seats have small flanges under which gaskets are fitted. Rubber gaskets supplied by the manufacturer are soon squeezed out, causing the seats to leak. Hard sheet packing will give better performance than rubber; and if cold water is to be pumped, sheet lead will give the best performance. When flanges cause a great deal of trouble, it will be necessary to fit new seats with a ground joint.

Frequently, valve stems shear off. To remedy this, cut the stem off the valve and turn a groove in the top of the valve for the spring to rest in. The stem is pinned to the guard at a sufficient height to allow proper opening of the valve; it then acts merely as a guide for the spring and as a limiting device for the valve. It will be necessary to fit a new stem because the old one will not be large enough to make a close fit in the guard.

Extreme care should be taken in assembling pumps after overhaul. Mark valves, valve seats, stems, and springs before removal, to make it easier to replace them in the proper order.

OPERATION OF RECIPROCATING PUMPS

Operating difficulties with reciprocating pumps will be encountered from time to time. Some of the most common causes of trouble and their remedies, are mentioned in the following sections.

Failure To Start

There may be times, after you have lined up the pump and cracked open the throttle valve, that the pump will not start. You may repeat the starting procedure, and determine that everything seems to be all right, but still the pump will not start. At this point, proceed as follows: Secure the pump. Check the suction, discharge, and auxiliary exhaust lines for a closed valve, or for a valve disk that has come off its stem. If no valves are closed, the water piston or the steam piston may be frozen, especially if the pump has been idle for some time.

This may be determined by jacking the pump with a bar.

CAUTION: Never attempt to jack a reciprocating pump unless you are certain that the throttle valve and the exhaust valve are closed tightly and the steam cylinder and steam chest drains are wide open.

If there is no excessive friction, disconnect the auxiliary valve stem from the operating gear without disturbing the adjustment of the tappet collars. Open the exhaust, suction, and discharge valves and then crack the throttle. Work the auxiliary piston valve by hand (the auxiliary valve should work freely). Should the pump still not start, secure steam and water end valves. Remove the steam valve chest to determine whether the main piston valve has overridden or stuck.

If the pump still cannot be started, a complete overhaul of the working parts of the steam end will be necessary.

Failure To Take Suction

When a reciprocating pump fails to take suction, the operation will be jerky. To correct this, proceed as follows: See that all stop and check valves in the suction line are open. Ensure that the suction line is free of all obstructions. If a reciprocating feed pump should become vapor bound, shift suction to a standby feedtank and open the vent valves in the valve chest cover and the discharge line to help cool the pump. Shift to the standby feed pump, if available, until the vapor-bound pump cools off.

Pumps having a suction lift, such as bilge pumps, may require priming before they will take suction. Salt water pumps can usually be primed from the sea by opening the sea suction for a short interval.

If failure to take suction is due to defective valves in the water end, the defects will have to be corrected before the pump will operate satisfactorily.

Loss Of Discharge Pressure

There are several reasons for a reciprocating pump to lose discharge pressure, some of the major reasons are:

1. Low steam pressure. Loss of steam pressure will cause the pump to slow down and will result in a loss of pump capacity and discharge pressure.

2. High back pressure. If the auxiliary exhaust pressure is allowed to become abnormally high, it will cause the pump to slow down and the discharge pressure will drop.

3. Worn piston rings. Leakage of steam by worn piston rings will cause the pump to operate erratically or even to stop. When worn rings are suspected, the steam end should be disassembled and the ring and piston measurements should be taken. If measurements are below the designed allowances, the rings will have to be renewed.

4. Defective valves. If a pump is operating normally and suddenly loses discharge pressure, a defective valve should be one of the first things to suspect. A large loss in efficiency will result from defective valves. If a pump races without increasing the discharge pressure, defective valves or air leaking into the suction line will probably be the cause.

5. Worn plunger packing. Another reason for a pump losing discharge pressure is worn packing on the water end plunger. The packing will wear, over a period of time, and the maximum discharge pressure from the pump will decrease accordingly; the only remedy is to renew the packing.

When you are trying to locate and correct troubles in a reciprocating pump, previous experience with a particular pump is always helpful. The first step should be to check all accessible parts. If the trouble cannot be located without disassembling the pump, the water end should be checked and determined to be satisfactory, before you remove any parts from the steam end.

CENTRIFUGAL PUMPS

Centrifugal pumps have, to a large extent, replaced direct-acting steam pumps for non-viscous liquid service aboard naval ships. Centrifugal pumps have several advantages over reciprocating pumps: They are simpler, more compact, lighter, and easily adapted to a high speed prime mover.

Centrifugal pumps also have disadvantages: They have a low suction power and must be primed in order to operate on a suction lift; they are also sensitive to variations in head and speed.

Centrifugal pumps are usually designed for specific operating conditions and will not give satisfactory results when their rated operating conditions are altered. Before installing any centrifugal pump, it is important to understand the principle of operation and design limitations of the specific pump.

OPERATION OF CENTRIFUGAL PUMPS

The details of operation for a centrifugal pump may vary from pump to pump. Pumps may look alike but this does not necessarily mean that they are operated in the same manner. Detailed instructions for operating a specific pump should be posted near the pump. Before operating the pump, the instructions should be carefully read. Read the label on all valves that apply to the pump. Check the markings on all piping that leads to or away from the pump and the pump's driving unit.

Many casualties that occur to pumps affect the speed of the ship. Many pump casualties, caused by improper operation, could be prevented by attentive watchstanding. Strict adherence to the manufacturer's instructions for starting, operating, and securing pumps will help prevent casualties.

Starting A Centrifugal Pump

The instructions contained in this chapter for the operation of pumps are general. All pumps cannot be covered because of the large number of makes and types of pumps installed aboard naval ships. Manufacturer's technical manuals are furnished with all but the simplest of pumps. These manuals contain detailed instructions concerning the specific pump and should be studied carefully before you attempt to operate the pump.

Prior to starting a centrifugal pump for the first time or after an overhaul, there are several items that should be checked. The coupling alignment must be carefully checked. Flexible couplings will take care of only very slight misalignment, usually about 0.002 to 0.004 inch. The exact figure can be found in the manufacturer's instructions. Excessive misalignment will cause the coupling to fail and may result in failure of the pump shaft or bearings.

If the pump is motor driven, the rotation of the unit should be checked. Most pumps have an arrow, on the pump casing, which indicates the proper direction of rotation.

Check all piping that pertains to the pump. During overhaul, most valves in the piping will have been closed. The lube oil system, the suction, discharge, vent, recirculating, and bypass valves must be lined up properly. An adequate supply of water must be available for the lube oil cooler; and inlet, outlet, and root valves should be checked.

When starting a steam-driven centrifugal pump, some of the important items to check or perform are as follows:

1. Check the level of oil in the sump tank or bearing housing. Fill oil cups or reservoirs, if fitted. If the pump is lubricated by a detached pump, open and adjust all valves in the discharge and suction lines.

2. Rotate the handle of the lube oil filter. Lubricate the linkage on the speed limiting governor.

3. Open the suction valve, the vent, and recirculating valves; open valves in gland water seal lines (if fitted). (The dis-

charge valve should be closed when starting centrifugal pumps.)

4. Open steam and exhaust root valves.

5. Check the suction pressure (if applicable).

6. Open all steam drains.

7. Open the turbine exhaust valve.

8. Open the bypass around the governor (if fitted).

9. Crack the turbine throttle valve.

10. Increase the steam chest pressure until the pump is turning fast enough to ensure adequate lube oil pressure.

11. Check packing glands for proper leak-off.

12. When the pump vent blows a solid stream of water, close the vent.

13. Close pump governor bypass and test the constant pressure governor.

14. When lube oil temperature reaches 90° F, open valve for cooling water to the lube oil cooler.

15. When ordered to put the pump (not fitted with a pressure governor) on the line, increase the pump discharge to the required amount by opening the throttle valve to necessary speed. If the pump is fitted with a constant pressure governor, set the governor to give the required discharge pressure.

16. When the pump is delivering the required discharge pressure, open the pump discharge valve.

NOTE: These items are riot necessarily listed in any proper order and all items do not apply to all steam-driven pumps.

Operating A Centrifugal Pump

When a pump has been started, it should not be left unattended. An experienced man should be on hand to check for abnormal operation. Frequent checks should be made on the temperature of the lube oil leaving the cooler and leaving each bearing. The suction and discharge pressures may become too high or too low. Packing glands may overheat and burn out.

The principal troubles that may occur with centrifugal pumps are:

1. Low discharge pressure. There are several reasons why a pump will not discharge at maximum capacity or pressure. The pump may be improperly primed, thus the proper quantity of liquid does not reach the pump casing. The speed of the pump may be too slow. On a turbine-driven pump, the speed limiting governor may be set too low, or the constant pressure governor may need adjusting. The pump may have mechanical defects such as worn wearing rings, worn bearings, a bent shaft, or a damaged impeller.

2. Loss of suction. If a pump has been operating satisfactorily and loses suction, air may be entering the suction line or packing glands. The suction strainer may have become clogged, or dirt or other foreign matter may have entered the impeller opening. In a main feed pump, the main feed booster pump may not be operating at its normal discharge pressure.

3. Excessive vibration. In a pump, excessive vibration may be due to one of the following causes: misalignment of the unit, a sprung foundation, worn impeller rings, worn bearings, a bent shaft, an improperly balanced impeller, or a broken impeller.

When putting a main feed pump on the line, make sure that the main feed booster pump is maintaining the required pressure. Boiler feed water is discharged under pressure from the main feed booster pump to the suction side of the main feed pump, which in turn discharges the feed water through the feed line to the boiler at a high pressure.

There are two sets of wearing rings in each stage, since the impellers are double entry. These wearing rings are designed with a minimum of clearance. These wearing rings have approximately the same clearance as the rings in a main feed booster pump, but the rotation of a main feed pump is five times as great as that of a main feed booster pump, so the possibility of seizure of the main feed pump wearing rings is much greater.

Water entering the suction of the main feed pump has its pressure reduced while passing through the entrance ports; since this water is at a temperature of about 240 F, this reduction in pressure might easily cause the water to flash into steam. It this occurs, the pump will become vapor bound, which prevents the flow of water through the pump and therefore prevents the removal of heat from the pump casing. A vapor-bound feed pump will require about 15 seconds to overheat, causing the wearing rings to seize.

The main feed booster pump discharge should be maintained at as near the designed value as possible. For an installation designed to operate at 50 psi of booster pressure, the main feed pump should not be turned over when there is less than 40 psi of booster pressure.

When main feed pumps are running, ensure that the oil temperature and pressure at the bearings are in accordance with the manufacturer's operating instructions. If a detached lube oil pump is provided, it will automatically cut in if the lube oil pressure fallsbelow a predetermined amount. If low lube oil pressure develops after the detached lube oil pump starts, shift to the standby unit, secure the faulty unit, and determine and correct the cause of low lube oil pressure. On installations where no detached lube oil pump is provided and low lube oil pressure occurs, shift immediately to the standby unit and do not operate the faulty pump until the proper lube oil pressure has been restored.

There is a common tendency to tighten packing glands too tightly. This causes the packing to burn and leads to scoring of the shaft sleeves. The packing glands should be adjusted so that a small amount of water is leaking out of the stuffing boxes. This water lubricates and cools the packing and packing gland. The packing gland should always be parallel to the face of the stuffing box and not cocked at an angle. If a stuffing box leaks exces-

sively, and it becomes necessary to tighten the gland, take up evenly on the gland bolts 1/2 turn. Wait a reasonable time, and if the leakage is still excessive, tighten the gland bolts another 1/2 turn. This procedure should be continued until there is only a trickle of water from the stuffing box.

When a main feed pump is running, do not change from hot to cold water or vice versa, unless there is an extreme emergency. Make periodic checks for vibration of the pump and driving unit. If vibration becomes excessive, stop the pump and investigate.

Securing A Centrifugal Pump

To secure a steam-driven centrifugal pump, proceed as follows:
1. Close the pump discharge valve.
2. Close the throttle valve.
3. Close the exhaust valve.
4. Close the suction valve.
5. Close the vent, recirculating, and gland sealing valves. (On some units, re-circulating and vent valves are locked open.)
6. Open the turbine casing drain.
7. Close the steam and exhaust root valves.
8. Close the turbine casing drain after the turbine is completely drained.

MAINTENANCE OF CENTRIFUGAL PUMPS

This chapter contains some of the information you must have in order to give proper care and maintenance to centrifugal pumps. Before attempting to repair any pump, the manufacturer's technical manual and the Material History for the pump should be studied carefully.

Inspection And Renewal Of Wearing Rings

The clearance between the impeller wearing ring and the casing wearing ring (fig. 4-4) must be maintained as shown in the manufacturer's plans. When clearances

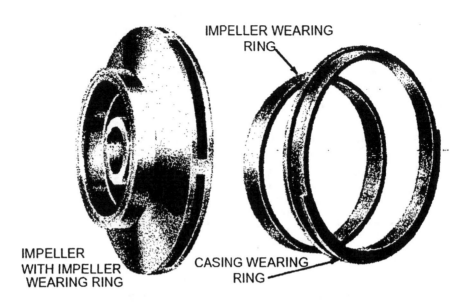

IMPELLER WEARING RING

IMPELLER WITH IMPELLER WEARING RING

CASING WEARING RING

75.281X

Figure 4-4. -Impeller, impeller wearing ring, and casing wearing ring for a centrifugal pump.

exceed the specified figures, the wearing rings must be replaced. On most ships, this job can be done by the ship's force but it requires the complete disassembly of the pump. All necessary information on disassembly of the unit, dimensions of the wearing rings, and reassembly of the pump can be found in the manufacturer's technical manual.

In deciding whether or not the wearing rings need renewing, the capacity of the pump and the discharge pressure of the pump must be taken into consideration. On low pressure pumps, the wearing ring diametral clearance may be 0.015 to 0.030 inch more than the designed amount without any appreciable effect on the pump's capacity. For pumps having a discharge pressure up to 75 psi, a wear of 0.030 to 0.050 inch is permissible.

The percentage of capacity loss, with a 0.030 inch wearing ring clearance, may be large with a small pump, but comparatively small with a large pump. For high pressure boiler feed pumps, the effect of increased wearing ring clearance is readily noticeable in the efficiency and maximum capacity of the pump. For high pressure pumps the wearing rings should be renewed when the clearance shown on the manufacturer's plans is exceeded by 100 percent. It is usually not considered necessary to renew wearing rings unless the wear is at least 0.015 inch. If a pump has to be disassembled because of some internal trouble, the wearing rings should be checked for clearance. Measure the outside diameter of the impeller wearing ring with an outside micrometer, and the inside diameter of the casing wearing ring with an inside micrometer; the difference between the two diameters will be the actual wearing ring diametral clearance. By checking the actual wearing ring clearance with the maximum allowable clearance, it can be decided whether to renew the rings before reassembling the pump.

The amount of work involved in disassembling the pump, the length of time the pump can be out of commission without affecting the ship, and whether or not a repair ship or other repair activity will be involved are some of the factors the engineer officer will take into consideration when determining whether to renew wearing rings.

For most small pumps, wearing rings are carried aboard as part of the ship's repair parts allowance. These may need only a slight amount of machining before they can be installed. For some pumps, such as main condensate, and main feed booster pumps, spare rotors are carried aboard. The new rotor can be installed and the old rotor sent to a repair activity for overhaul. Overhauling a rotor usually includes renewing the wearing rings, bearings, and the shaft packing sleeve.

Bearing Maintenance

Pump bearings must receive approximately the same tests, inspections, and maintenance as bearings installed in other units of naval machinery. Pump bearings must be supplied with an adequate amount of oil at the right temperature and of the viscosity designated for that particular pump. The manufacturer's technical manual contains information on lubrication of each pump.

Thrust bearings should be examined quarterly. The condition of the bearing and the position of the rotor should be checked. When checking the rotor position, allowance should be made for expansion of the shaft from cold to hot condition. There are many types of thrust bearings installed in pumps; and the manufacturer's technical manual should be checked before attempting disassembly of any thrust bearing.

Journal bearings should be checked at least every 6 months. The condition of the journal and the bearing surface should be checked and any deficiencies corrected. Lead readings shouldbe taken and bearing clearances should be maintained as shown in the manufacturer's plans.

Water-lubricated bearings are installed in main condensate pumps and main circulating pumps. In main condensate pumps, the bearing is located in the casing, between the first-stage and second-stage suction compartments, where it also serves as an interstage seal. Vertical movement of the bearing is prevented by shoulders in the casing; and a stop pin prevents angular movement. During normal operation of the pump, the bearing is lubricated by a constant flow of water through the bearing which is maintained as a result of the pressure differential between the two suction compartments.

In main circulating pumps (fig. 4-5), the water-lubricated bearing is located immediately above the propeller and is designed for a radial load only. The bearing is held in place by shoulders in the casing and is lubricated by the flow of water through the pump.

A number of materials have been used for water-lubricated bearings, such as leaded bronze, graphited bronze, lignum vitae, and Bearium; most water-lubricated bearings are now made of rubber or phenolic composition.

The condition of water-lubricated bearings should be checked frequently to guard against excessive wear which would cause shaft misalignment and possible bearing wear or shaft breakage.

Ball and roller bearings are used in many shipboard pumps, especially in-small pumps, and in main condensate, main feed booster, and lube oil service pumps. These bearings must be handled as carefully as any other piece of precision equipment. The following precautions will aid in proper bearing maintenance:

1.   Do not remove the bearing from its container until you are ready to install it.

2.   Be certain that the journal, housing, or any other mating part is of the correct dimensions.

3.   Avoid damage during handling; do not drop the bearing; keep dirt and moisture away from the bearing, shaft, and housing.

4.   Use proper tools for removing the old bearing and installing the new bearing.

5.   Use the correct lubricant and the proper amount. After assembly the journal should be rotated by hand to ensure that there is no undue friction.

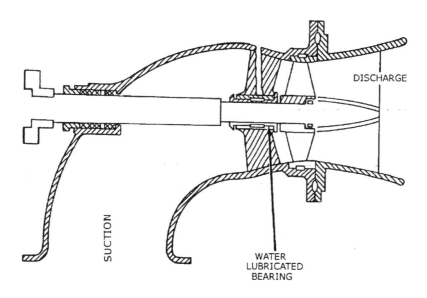

Figure 4-5.- Main condenser circulating pump, showing internal water-lubricared bearing.

96.15

In rolling contact bearings, the journal is supported by the races and rolling elements, rather than the oil film; however, lubrication still plays an important part in the operation because it dissipates heat and prevents corrosion. The oil film also helps prevent foreign matter from entering the bearing. Enough grease or oil should be supplied to provide a protective film over the bearing parts; using an excessive 'amount of lubricant will cause it to churn and the bearing will overheat.

When a roller or ball bearing fails in service, it must be renewed as it cannot be repaired. The replacement bearing must be carefully installed if it is to give satisfactory service.

Lubricating Systems

Lack of lubrication or improper lubrication is a major cause of pump failure. Before a pump is started, the level of oil in the sump should be checked-not only for the amount of oil, but also for the quality of oil it contains. If water is found in the oil sump, check for leakage from turbine glands, a leaky oil cooler, or any other possible source of water contamination. The oil filters or strainers must be checked frequently; in those with edge filtration (such as in the Cuno type filter), the sediment, which will collect in the bottom of the filter, must be cleaned out frequently. Housings of grease-lubricated bearings should be checked occasionally to ensure that they are free of water, dirt, and other foreign matter. If water is found in the bearing housing, it should be traced to its source. The frequency with which grease is added to a bearing must be determined by the type of service and the effectiveness of the grease seals.

When starting a pump, check the oil pressure and the flow of oil to all bearings. Make sure that the lube oil pump is discharging at the designed pressure. Ensure that cooling water is flowing through the oil cooler and that all air is vented from the cooler. It may be necessary to vent the lube oil system. To do this, open the vent on the highest point in the lube oil system and close the vent when oil appears.

When water or other foreign matter is found in a lube oil system, the unit should not be operated until the system has been drained, cleaned, and filled with the proper quantity and quality of oil.

Replacing Pump Rotors

Pumps, like all machinery, in time, will need overhauling. Much of the work on pumps involves removing the rotor from the casing. To renew wearing rings, bearings, packing, sleeves, or impellers, the casing must be removed and the rotor lifted out.

In order to disassemble a main feed pump the following procedure is recommended:

1.   Close and wire shut all suction, discharge, vent, and recirculating valves. Drain water from the casing.

2.   Remove all suction, discharge, vent, and recirculating lines that will interfere with lifting the casing and rotor.

3.   Remove the bearing caps and the bearings (journal and thrust).

4.   Disconnect the coupling between the turbine and pump.

5.   Remove the packing glands and the packing.

6.   Remove the pump casing horizontal joint bolts.

7.   Break the horizontal casing joint by tightening the jack screws.

8.   Attach the lifting gear to the upper half of the casing (eyebolts are provided for this purpose).

9. Lift the upper half of the casing until it is clear of the rotor. Change the lifting gear and swing the upper casing half clear of the pump.

10. Attach cables around the shaft at both ends, making certain that you do not lift on a journal surface, and lift the rotor out of the lower half of the casing.

11. The rotor can then be moved to a location where it can be disassembled. In order for you to have access to all rotor parts, the rotor should be placed on a workbench, or if available, two wooden sawhorses.

Remove all rotor parts in the sequence and in the manner recommended by the manufacturer.

It may be necessary to heat the impellers in order to remove them. If so, warm the impeller evenly all around, while keeping the shaft as cool as possible.

When the rotor parts are disassembled, the shaft should be checked carefully. The journal surfaces should be checked for burrs or nicks. If a lathe is available, the shaft can be swung in the lathe, and with a dial indicator, you can determine whether the shaft is bent or the journals are out of round. The journal surfaces can be measured with an outside micrometer to determine whether there is wear. If the journals are worn or out of round, they can be built up and machined to the designed diameter, at a repair activity. If the wearing rings are to be renewed, they will have to be fitted either in the ship's machine shop, or at a repair activity.

Before starting to reassemble the rotor, make sure that all parts are clean and free of burrs (especially the faces of the impeller and the sleeves).

The oil clearances of the journal and thrust bearings, the running clearance of the wearing rings, the clearance between the impeller and diaphragm bushing, and clearance between the shaft sleeve and stuffing box bushing should be within the limits indicated in the manufacturer's technical manual.

Before lowering the rotor, roll in the lower half of the journal bearings. Clean all dirt and foreign matter from the lower half of the casing. A new parting flange gasket should be used to avoid leaks, as internal leaks will lower the efficiency and maximum capacity of the pump.

Attach the lifting gear and lower the rotor into the casing. Make sure that all stationary rotor parts: diaphragms, casing rings, and stuffing box bushings will enter their respective fits in the casing without binding. If force has to be applied to the rotor parts, in order for them to enter the casing, remove the rotor and check all parts for dirt and burrs.

When the rotor is in place, lower the upper half of the casing. Ensure that the casing fits over the rotor easily. If it does not, remove the upper casing half and examine it for dirt and burrs. When the upper and lower casing halves contact each other properly, insert the casing dowels. Next, tighten the parting flange nuts, tighten them evenly by going over them several times. Assemble the thrust bearing, then place the upper half of the bearings in position and bolt the two halves of each together. Adjust the flingers; they should be close to the face of the bearings but MUST not rub. Tighten the flinger setscrews and close up the bearings by placing the caps over them and tighting the bolts. Take a reading on the thrust bearing clearance.

The pump shaft and turbine shaft MUST be in correct alignment. For information on pump alignment, refer to the manufacturer's technical manual

All water lines MUST be in place and tightened before you attempt to align the unit, otherwise tightening the lines may cause misalignment of the unit. Pack the stuffing boxes with the proper packing; then the unit is ready to be tested.

Rotate the pump several times, by hand, before steam is cut into the driving unit. Ensure that there is no undue binding or friction.

The procedure for replacing a main conden-sate pump rotor or a main feed booster pump rotor is similar. These pumps are usually vertically mounted and the rotor can be disassembled without disturbing the driving unit. The procedure is as follows:

1. Obtain the applicable manufacturer's technical manual and blueprints. Study the construction details and procedures for assembly and disassembly. Note the manufacturer's data on wearing ring clearances, bearing clearances, and other necessary dimensions. Check the Machinery History Card

2. Remove the new rotor from its storage place. Clean and inspect the new rotor, take all necessary measurements.

3. Assemble all necessary lifting gear and tools, including special tools.

4. Remove the nuts at the parting flange and remove the casing half. Take off the bearing cap, unbolt the bearing housing, disconnect the coupling, and lift out the old rotor.

5. Inspect the interior of the casing, clean all flanges and make new gaskets. (New gaskets should be used on all flanges as any leakage through a main condensate pump flange will result in a loss of vacuum in the main condenser.)

6. After the cleaning and inspecting are done, lower the new rotor into place.

7. Place the casing in position and tighten the parting flange nuts. If the casing binds or does not fit properly, remove the casing and correct the trouble.

8. When the casing has been secured in place, the rotor should be rotated by hand to ensure that there is no binding or undue friction.

9. Reassemble the bearing housing and connect the coupling. If the pump still turns freely, the unit is ready to be tested by steam (or motor). If all conditions are satisfactory, bring the pump up to operating speed and pressure. When the pump is used for the first time, it should be kept under close observation for several hours and should not be considered ready for unlimited operation until it has carried the required load with the ship under way.

Prepare a work request for the necessary repairs to the defective rotor. All necessary details, including balancing, should be written up and the rotor taken to the appropriate repair activity. All pump and driving unit rotating parts are balanced dynamically for all speeds from at rest to 125 percent of rated speed. The parts are usually dynamically balanced on balancing machines, generally available on tenders and repair ships and at all naval shipyards.

On ships with adequate shop facilities, pump rotors may be overhauled on board. The rotor should be taken to the machine shop and dismantled. The parts should be taken off the shaft in the sequence recommended by the manufacturer. When the parts have been removed from the shaft, the shaft should be checked in the same manner as previously described in this chapter for shafts of main feed pump rotors.

If the shaft is not bent or out of round, the parts can be reinstalled on the shaft, using new parts as needed. Ball bearings can be shrunk or pressed on the shaft. The best practice is to heat the bearing, in an oil bath, to about 200° F (but not exceeding this temperature), then slip it over the journal and position it by means of the locknut. The locknut can be tightened as the bearing cools.

Wearing rings should be given the clearance recommended by the manufacturer. When the rotor is reassembled, it should be properly stowed, so as to be ready for use when needed.

Generally, it is more difficult to replace main lube oil service pump rotors than rotors in other types of pumps. The driving unit must be removed before the liquid end can be disassembled. With the drive unit removed, the pump rotor and rotor housing can be disassembled without removing the mountings or the main lube oil connections.

Under normal operating conditions, the rotors are completely covered with oil, which cuts rotor wear to a minimum. Therefore, the rotors may give years of satisfactory service without repairs. In some instances, rotor failure has been due to normal wear, air trapped in the casing, or entrance of dirt, wood, or metal objects into the casing. To replace a defective rotor, proceed as follows:

On a turbine-driven unit, remove the drive unit by breaking the steam and exhaust lines, disconnecting the coupling, removing the bolts which secure the spacing frame to the pump casing, attaching the lifting gear, and lifting the drive unit off intact.

To disassemble the liquid end (fig. 4-6), first remove the lower coupling half, the packing gland, and the upper casing head.

The rotors will then be exposed and can be withdrawn. As the rotors are lifted out of their housings, the idlers must be supported; the pump is constructed in such a manner that only the housings hold the rotors in mesh. With the rotors removed, the housings are accessible. The housings fit snugly in the bore of the casing and are separated by a spacer ring. They are positioned axially by jam screws, which bear on the casing heads; and circumferentially by guide pins, which are fitted individually to ensure alignment of the housing bores. The guide pins are secured by pipe plugs. Before the rotor housings can be removed, it is necessary to take out the housing guide pins, the outer ends of which are drilled and tapped for the application of a pulling tool. Because these guide pins are fitted parts, each pin must be marked as it is withdrawn, so that it can be replaced properly.

Before the reassembling operations are started, all parts of the pump should be carefully inspected and cleaned. Also, it should be definitely ascertained that the settings of the lower housing jam screws are correct (check the manufacturer's technical manual or blueprint).

When reassembling the pump, lower the bottom housing, the spacer, and the upper housing into place separately. Ensure that each part seats firmly and that the guide pin slot in each housing registers with the pin hole in the casing. The special tool used for pulling the housings can also be used in assembling them. Next, install the housing guide pins and their securing plugs. If new housings are installed, the bores must be carefully aligned and new guide pins fitted to maintain alignment. The jam screws may then be set up in the upper housing.

Insert the rotors and turn them by hand to see that they are free and do not bind. Binding of the rotors is an almost certain indication that the housing bores are not in line, or that the guide pins or the housings, or both, have not been properly installed. Install the upper casing head,

96.16

Figure 4-6. - Rotor assembly for a lube oil service pump.

making sure that the thrust plate and the seal bushing are in place and that the latter is secured by the stop pin provided for that purpose.

When a pump is assembled at the factory, the locating caps on the idlers are set up to establish the proper running positions of the idlers with reference to the power rotor, and are then secured by riveting. So long as a set of rotors remains intact, readjustment of the locating cap settings will rarely be found necessary. Even over long periods of service, wear of the hardened contact surfaces will be negligible.

Whenever new rotors are installed, the proper locating cap settings must be established. The proper cap settings are such that the lower end surfaces of all three rotors will lie in a common plane when the rotors are properly meshed and the idlers are located centrally with respect to end play in the power rotor.

The cap settings must be established before the rotors are installed, but the rotors should be inserted in one of the housings for the adjustments, to ensure proper meshing. A tapped hole is provided in the base of each cap, so that the pulling

tool, or some other suitably threaded implement, can be used to jack the cap into position. After the settings have been established, the caps should be riveted into place; this entails drilling the shaft ends for the rivets. Rivet holes are provided in the caps of all idlers supplied by the factory.

Shaft-driven lube oil pumps are of the same size and design as the steam-driven pumps, but differ in their mountings and drive details.

Some pumps are hooked up to the main shaft through a sprocket and chain drive so that they operate continuously while the shaft is turning over. These pumps are designed with vertical shaft and horizontal shaft units.

On ships built since World War II, the attached lube oil pump is driven from the main reduction gear by an assembly of bevel and spur gears. The driving connection is made by a pinion, mounted on a hub, that is attached to the lower, low pressure, low speed pinion quill shaft coupling. The pump is located on the inboard side, at the after end of the main reduction gear housing.

Before a chain-driven pump can be disassembled, the drive must be completely dismantled as follows:

1. Disconnect the oil lines leading to and from the chain housing.

2. Remove the chain cover.

3. Break and remove the chain. The manufacturer supplies a special tool and detailed instructions for breaking the chain.

4. Remove the lower section of the chain casing from its supporting frame.

5. For a vertical unit, remove the frame which supports the chain casing and houses the drive gears. The drive shaft mounting need not be disturbed for this operation.

With the driving mechanism out of the way, the horizontal pump can be dismantled in place, provided there is sufficient clearance for the withdrawal of the rotors. The vertical unit must be detached from its base and transferred to a location where both ends of the casing are accessible so that the rotors can be withdrawn.

If space permits, the rotors can be withdrawn from either end of the casing, but it is easier to withdraw them from the outer end (the end away from the drive unit), because this method does not require the removal of the inner casing head. (Removal of the outer casing head is a necessary step in the disassembling operation.)

Removal of the rotors from the outer end of the casing entails removing the sprocket, removing the outer casing head, freeing the rotors, and withdrawing them.

Pump Control Devices

Turbine-driven centrifugal pumps are fitted with devices to control or limit the speed of the unit, or to regulate the discharge pressure of the unit.

Speed limiting governors are set to give a rated speed at rated load conditions. With the governor properly set, the turbine speed should not exceed the rated speed by more than 5 percent, for any condition of load. If the governor will not function within the prescribed limit, it must be overhauled, and the cause of faulty operation located and corrected. Speed limiting governors should be tested at least every 3 months.

To set a governor of this type, remove the governor lever, and the governor cover. The governor spring will then be accessible.

If it is desired to increase the maximum speed of the unit, the tension on the governor spring must be increased by tightening the adjusting nut. With increased spring tension, more centrifugal force will be required to move the weights outward-which in turn moves the sleeve outward against one end of the governor lever (moving the other end of the governor lever inward), closing down on the poppet valve, and decreasing the amount of steam flow to the turbine.

Decreasing the tension on the governor spring will allow the governor weights to move outward with less centrifugal force,

thus decreasing the maximum speed of the unit.

Very little wear is experienced in a speed limiting governor; however, preventive maintenance is required. The governor must be kept clean. Dirt or other foreign matter can foul the spring, and thus require more force to move the weights, which will allow the pump to over-speed. Rust on the governor lever fulcrum pin will cause the lever to bind and not function properly. All pins in the linkage and the valve stem must be kept free of paint, rust, and dirt so that the linkage can move freely. Occasionally, a test should be made to determine whether the poppet valve is leaking. The test may be made by pushing the valve onto its seat by hand. If the valve is leaking the turbine will continue to rotate.

Turbine-driven main feed pumps and fire pumps are fitted with constant pressure governors which control the discharge pressure of the unit by automatically controlling the amount of steam admitted to the turbine.

The instructions for operation, care, and repair of constant pressure governors contained in this chapter are general for all types of governors. For specific instructions, consult the applicable manufacturer's technical manual.

One of the most common causes of trouble with a constant pressure governor is sluggishness due to dirt or foreign matter interfering with free movement of the working parts. To correct sluggishness, the governor must be taken apart and cleaned as follows:

1. Unscrew the connector union, remove the bottom nuts from the bolts holding the superstructure to the top cap, and then lift off the superstructure above the lower diaphragm. (When the superstructure is reassembled, care must be taken that the diaphragm stem, diaphragm stem cap, and diaphragm disk are put back in proper position. Make sure that the connecting rods are free and do not bind in their guides.)

2. Unscrew the controlling valve with the special wrench provided for this purpose,

remove the controlling valve and controlling valve spring.

3. Remove the top cap and lift out the piston and cylinder liner. Remove the bottom cap and take out the main valve and main valve spring.

4. Clean all parts thoroughly. See that the main valve and the controlling valve seat properly and that the piston rings are free in their grooves. Clean the seat for the cylinder liner so that the cylinder liner does not project above the top flange of the main body. Clean the bore of the main valve guide and stem. If necessary, grind in the main valve seat and disk. Make certain that the stem of the controlling valve does not project above the diaphragm seat. The correct clearance between the controlling valve stem and the diaphragm is 0.001 to 0.002 inch.

When renewing gaskets and diaphragms of governors, be sure to use only parts made by the manufacturer of the governor. The diaphragm must be of the correct thickness and installed WITHOUT gaskets. Do not use graphite or other such substances on gaskets.

The control valve is another frequent cause of trouble in a Leslie pump governor. Steam, passing through the control valve, is continuously throttled; and the valve is subjected to considerable erosion (wire drawing). The control valve and control valve seat should be inspected frequently. When reassembling the control valve or installing a new one, it is very important to maintain the correct clearance between the control valve stem and the lower diaphragm. If the clearance is excessive, the lower diaphragm cannot fully open the control valve, and the pump capacity is reduced. If there is not enough clearance, the diaphragm will hold the control valve open and the pump cannot be stopped without closing the throttle valve. It is also necessary that there be no steam leakage through the control valve or under the control valve bushing because the leaking steam will hold the main valve open, allowing steam to flow to the turbine.

Faulty governor operation is sometimes due to the piston rings wearing grooves in the cylinder liner. The grooves will limit the travel of the main valve and reduce the capacity of the pump, or will cause failure of the governor. Whenever a constant pressure governor is disassembled, the liner should be carefully checked; and if it is grooved, it should be renewed.

Control valve springs should be inspected frequently. If the spring breaks or is weak, it cannot close the control valve, which allows a full flow of steam to the turbine.

SAFETY PRECAUTIONS FOR OPERATING PUMPS

1. Do not operate a pump with a defective overspeed trip, speed limiting governor, or speed regulating governor. If, in an emergency, a main feed pump or fire pump must be operated with a defective constant pressure governor, a man MUST be stationed at the throttle valve of the pump to regulate the discharge pressure.

2. Ensure that overspeed trips, where fitted, are set to shut off steam to the pump when the rated speed is exceeded by 10 percent.

3. See that speed limiting governors are set to limit the speed of the unit at not more than 105 percent of rated speed.

4. Check all pump control devices at least once each quarter, and more often if so ordered by proper authority.

ELECTRIC MOTOR AND GENERATOR REPAIR

CONTENTS

Page

I. TROUBLESHOOTING DATA FOR GENERATORS AND MOTORS ... 1
   Section I. DC Generators ... 1
      1. Failure to Build up Voltage ... 1
      2. Output Voltage too Low ... 1
      3. Output Voltage too High ... 1
      4. Armature Overheats ... 1
      5. Field Coils Overheat ... 2
      6. Sparking at Brushes ... 2
   Section II. DC Motors ... 2
      7. Failure to Start ... 2
      8. Stops After Running a Short Time ... 2
      9. Attempts to Start, but Overload Relays Trip Out ... 2
     10. Runs too Slow ... 3
     11. Runs too Fast Under Load ... 3
     12. Sparking at Brushes ... 3
     13. Overheating ... 3
   Section III. AC Generators ... 3
     14. Noisy Operation ... 3
     15. Overheating ... 3
     16. No Output Voltage ... 3
     17. Output Voltage Unsteady ... 4
     18. Output Voltage too High ... 4
     19. Frequency Incorrect or Fluctuating ... 4
     20. Voltage Hunting ... 4
     21. Stator Overheats in Spots ... 4
     22. Field Overheating ... 4
     23. Alternator Produces Shock When Touched ... 4
   Section IV. AC Induction Motors ... 4
     24. Failure to Start ... 4
     25. Noisy Operation ... 4
     26. Overheating ... 5
   Section V. AC Wound Rotor Motors ... 5
     27. Runs Slow with External Resistance Cutout ... 5
   Section VI. AC Synchronous Motors ... 5
     28. Failure to Start ... 5
     29. Runs Slow ... 5
     30. Failure to Pull into Step ... 5
     31. No Field Excitation ... 5
     32. Pulls Out of Step, or Trips Breakers ... 6
     33. Hunting ... 6
     34. Stator Overheats in Spots ... 6
     35. Field Overheats ... 6
     36. Overheating ... 6
   Section VII. AC Repulsion Induction Motors ... 6
     37. Failure to Start ... 6
     38. Runs Slow ... 7
     39. Overheating ... 7
     40. Noisy Operation ... 7
     41. Motor Produces Shock when Touched ... 7

continued ....

CONTENTS

		Page
Section VIII. AC Split-Phase, Capacitor-Start, and Transformer-Capacitor Motors		7
42. Failure to Start		7
43. Overheating		7
44. Noisy Operation		8
II. TROUBLESHOOTING DATA FOR DC AND AC CONTROLLERS		9
Section I. DC Controllers		9
45. Failure to Close		9
46. Failure to Open		9
47. Sluggish Operation		9
48. Erratic Operation (Unwanted openings and closures, and failure of overload protection)		9
49. Overheating of Coils		10
50. Contacts Welded Together		10
51. Overheating of Contacts		10
52. Excessive Arcing of Contacts		10
53. Pitting or Corroding of Contacts		11
Section II. AC Controllers		11
54. Failure to Close		11
55. Failure to Open		11
56. Sluggish Operation		11
57. Erratic Operation (Unwanted openings and closures, and failure of overload protection)		12
58. Overheating of Coils		12
59. Contacts Welded Together		12
60. Overheating or Contacts		12
61. Arcing at Contacts		13
62. Pitting or Corroding of Contacts		13
63. Noisy Operation (Hum or Chatter)		13
64. Vibration After Repairs		13

———

ELECTRIC MOTOR AND GENERATOR REPAIR

I. TROUBLESHOOTING DATA FOR GENERATORS AND MOTORS

Section I. DC GENERATORS

I. Failure to Build up Voltage

Probable cause	*Remedy*
Voltmeter not operating	Check output voltage with separate voltmeter. Replace voltmeter.
Open field resistor	Repair or replace resistor.
Open field circuit	Check coils for open and loose connections. Replace the defective coil or coils. Tighten or solder loose connections.
Absence of residual magnetism in a self-excited generator.	Flash the field.
Dirty commutator	Clean or dress commutator.
High mica	Undercut mica.
Brushes not making proper contact	Free, if binding in holders. Replace and reseat if worn.
Newly seated brushes not contacting sufficient area on the commutator.	Run in by reducing load and use a brush-seating stone.
Armature shorted internally, or to ground	Remove, test, and repair or replace.
Grounded or shorted field coil	Test, and repair or replace.
Shorted filtering capacitor	Replace.
Open filter choke	Replace.
Open ammeter shunt	Replace ammeter and shunt.
Broken brush shunts or pigtails	Replace brushes.

2. Output Voltage too Low

Probable cause	*Remedy*
Prime mover speed too low	Check speed with tachometer. Adjust governor on prime mover.
Brushes not seated properly	Run in with partial load, use brush-seating stone.
Commutator is dirty or film is too heavy	Clean, or if film is too heavy, replace brushes with a complete set of proper grade.
Field resistor not properly adjusted	Adjust field strength. Tighten all connections. Make shim adjustment.
Reversed field coil or armature connection	Check and connect properly.

3. Output Voltage Too High

Probable cause	*Remedy*
Prime mover speed too high	Check speed with tachometer. Adjust governor on prime mover.
Faulty voltage regulator	Adjust or replace.

4. Armature Overheats

Probable cause	*Remedy*
Overloaded	Check meter readings against nameplate ratings. Reduce load.
Excessive brush pressure	Adjust pressure or replace tension springs.
Couplings not alined	Aline units properly

Probable cause	Remedy
End bells improperly positioned	Assemble correctly
Bent shaft	Straighten or replace
Armature coil shorted	Repair or replace armature
Armature rubbing or striking poles	Check for bent shaft, loose or worn bearings. Straighten and realine shaft. Replace bearings, tighten pole pieces, or replace armature.
Clogged air passages (poor ventilation)	Clean equipment
Repeated changes in load of great magnitude. (Improper design for the application).	Generator should be used with a steady load application.
Unequal brush tension	Equalize brush tension
Broken shunts or pigtails	Replace brushes
Open in field rheostat	Repair or replace rheostat

5. Field Coils Overheat

Probable cause	Remedy
Shorted or grounded coils	Repair or replace
Clogged air passages (poor ventilation)	Clean equipment. Remove obstructions.
Overload (compound generator)	Check meter reading against nameplate rating. Reduce load.

6. Sparking at Brushes

Probable cause	Remedy
Overload	Check meter readings against nameplate ratings. Reduce load.
Brushes off neutral plane	Adjust brush rigging.
Dirty brushes and commutator	Clean brushes and commutator.
High mica	Undercut mica.
Rough or eccentric commutator	Resurface commutator.
Open circuit in the armature	Repair or replace armature.
Grounded, open- or short-circuited field winding	Repair or replace defective coil or coils.
Insufficient brush pressure	Adjust or replace tension springs.
Brushes sticking in the holders	Clean holders. Sand brushes.

Section II.   DC MOTORS

7. Failure to Start

Probable cause	Remedy
Open circuit in the control	Check for open. Replace open resistor or fuse.
Low supply voltage	Check with voltmeter and apply proper voltage.
Frozen bearing	Replace bearing and recondition shaft.
Overload	Reduce load or use larger motor.
Excessive friction	Check for air gap, bent shaft, loose or worn bearings, misalined end bells. Straighten shaft, replace bearings, tighten pole pieces, aline end bells.

8. Stops After Running a Short Time

Probable cause	Remedy
Failure of supply voltage	Apply proper voltage, replace fuses, or reset overload relay.
Overload	Check meter readings against nameplate ratings. Reduce load.
Ambient temperature too high	Ventilate space to reduce ambient temperature.
Overload relays set too low for application	Adjust relays for the application.

9. Attempts to Start, But Overload Relays Trip Out

Probable cause	Remedy
Motor field weak or non-existent	Check field circuit. Repair or replace defective field coils. Tighten all connections.
Overload	Check meter readings against nameplate ratings. Replace motor with one suitable to the application.
Relays adjusted too low for the application	Adjust relays for the application.

10. Runs too Slow

Probable cause	Remedy
Line voltage low	Apply proper voltage.
Bushes ahead of neutral plane	Adjust brush rigging.
Overload	Check meter reading against nameplate readings. Reduce load.

11. Runs too Fast under Load

Probable cause	Remedy
Weak field	Check field circuit. Replace open coils or open starter resistors.
Line voltage too high	Reduce line voltage.
Brushes off adjustment with neutral plane	Adjust brush rigging.

12. Sparking at Brushes

Probable cause	Remedy
Same as dc generator (par. 6)	Same as dc generator (par. 6).

13. Overheating

Probable cause	Remedy
Same as dc generator (par. 4 and 5)	Same as dc generator (par. 4 and 5).

Section III. AC GENERATORS

14. Noisy Operation

Probable cause	Remedy
Unbalanced load	Balance load.
Coupling loose or misalined	Reline coupling and tighten.
Improper air gap	Check for bent shaft, loose or worn bearings. Straighten and realine shaft. Replace bearings.
Loose laminations	Tighten bolts. Dip in varnish and bake.

15. Overheating

Probable cause	Remedy
Overloaded	Check meter readings against nameplate ratings. Reduce load.
Unbalanced load	Balance load.
Open load-line fuse	Replace fuse.
Restricted ventilation	Clean, and remove obstructions to ventilation.
Rotor winding short-circuited, open-circuited, or grounded.	Check, and replace defective coil or coils.
Stator winding short-circuited, open-circuited, or grounded.	Check, and replace defective coil or coils.
Bearings	Check for worn, loose, dry, or overlubricated bearings. Replace worn or loose bearings, lubricate dry bearings, relieve overlubrication.

16. No Output Voltage

Probable cause	Remedy
Stator coils open- or short-circuited	Check, and replace defective coil or coils.
Rotor coils open- or short-circuited	Check, and replace defective coil or coils.
Shorted sliprings	Disconnect field coils and check ring-insulation resistance with megger. Repair.
Internal moisture	Check with megger and dry windings.
No dc voltage at the slipring brushes. (No dc exciter voltage.)	Check for defective switch or blown fuse in exciter feeder lines. Repair switch or replace fuses. Check feeder cables for opens or shorts. Repair connections or replace cables. Refer to FAILURE TO BUILD UP VOLTAGE (par. 1).
Voltmeter defective	Check with a voltmeter known to be working properly. Replace.
Ammeter shunt open	Replace ammeter and shunt.

17. Output Voltage Unsteady

Probable cause	Remedy
Poor commutation at sliprings	Clean sliprings and brushes. Reseat brushes.
Loose terminal connections	Clean and tighten all connections and contacts.
Maladjusted voltage regulator and speed governor	Readjust speed governor and voltage regulator.

18. Output Voltage too High

Probable cause	Remedy
Overspeeding	Adjust speed-governing device.
Overexcited	Adjust voltage regulator.
Delta-connected stator open on one leg	Remake connection, repair or replace defective coil or coils.

19. Frequency Incorrect or Fluctuating

Probable cause	Remedy
Speed incorrect or fluctuating	Adjust speed-governing device.
Dc excitation fluctuating	Adjust belt tension of exciter generator.

20. Voltage Hunting

Probable cause	Remedy
External field resistance in total out position	Readjust resistance.
Voltage regulator contacts dirty	Clean and reset contact points.

21. Stator Overheats in Spots

Probable cause	Remedy
Short-circuited phase winding	Check and replace defective coils.
Rotor off center. (Improper air gap.)	Check for bent shaft, loose or worn bearings. Straighten and realine shaft. Replace bearings.
Unbalanced winding circuits	Balance winding circuits.
Loose winding connections	Tighten winding connections.
Wrong phase polarity connections	Correct connections for proper phase polarity.

22. Field Overheating

Probable cause	Remedy
Shorted field coil or coils	Check and replace defective coil or coils.
Dc excitation current too high	Reduce exciter current by adjusting dc voltage regulator.
Clogged air passages (poor ventilation)	Clean equipment. Remove obstructions.

23. Alternator Produces Shock when Touched

Probable cause	Remedy
Reversed stator field coil	Check polarity. Make correction to connections.
Static charges or grounded stator field coil	Check generator frame-ground connection or connections, clean and tighten. Repair or replace stator field coil.

Section IV.   AC INDUCTION MOTORS

24. Failure to Start

Probable cause	Remedy
Circuit breaker or fuse open	Check for grounds. Close breaker or replace fuse.
Overload relay open	Wait until motor cools and relay closes.
Low supply voltage	Apply correct voltage.
Stator or rotor windings open or shorted	Check and replace shorted coil or coils.
Winding grounded	Check and replace grounded coil or coils.
Overload	Check meter readings against nameplate ratings. Reduce or install larger motor.

25. Noisy Operation

Probable cause	Remedy
Unbalanced load or coupling misalinement	Balance load and check alinement.
Air gap not uniform	Center rotor by replacing bearing.
Lamination loose	Tighten bolts. Dip in varnish and bake (chapter 4, par. 70). Repeat several times.
Coupling loose	Tighten.

26. Overheating

Probable cause	Remedy
Overloaded	Check meter readings against nameplate ratings. Reduce load.
Electrical unbalance	Balance supply voltage.
Open fuse	Replace line fuse.
Restricted ventilation	Clean. Remove obstructions.
Rotor winding shorted, open, or grounded	Check and replace defective coil or coils.
Stator winding shorted, open, or grounded	Check and replace defective coil or coils.
Bearings	Check for worn, loose, dry, or overlubricated bearings. Replace worn or loose bearings, lubricate dry bearings, relieve overlubrication.

Section V. AC WOUND ROTOR MOTORS

27. Runs Slow with External Resistance Cutout

Probable cause	Remedy
Cables to control box have insufficient current-carrying capacity.	Replace with larger cables.
Open circuits in rotor, cables, or controls	Clean, remake connections, and repair.
Excessive brush sparking	Clean sliprings and reseat brushes.

Section VI. AC SYNCHRONOUS MOTORS

28. Failure to Start

Probable cause	Remedy
Open fuse	Replace fuse.
Faulty starter	Check and repair or replace faulty contacts or contactor coils.
Low supply voltage	Apply correct voltage.
Bearings	Check for bent shaft or worn, loose, dry, or overlubricated bearings. Replace and realine bent shaft. Replace worn and loose bearings, lubricate dry bearings, relieve overlubrication.
Overloaded	Check meter readings against nameplate ratings. Reduce load or install larger motor.
Stator coil open or shorted	Repair or replace coil or coils.
Field exciter current is being applied	Make sure that field contactors are open, and that field-discharge resistors are connected.

29. Runs Slow

Probable cause	Remedy
Overloaded	Check meter readings against nameplate. Reduce load or install larger motor.
Low supply voltage	Apply correct voltage.
Field excited too soon	Adjust time-delay relay so that exciter current will not be applied until rotor reaches synchronous speed.

30. Failure to Pull into Step

Probable cause	Remedy
No field excitation. Open rotor coils. Exciter inoperative. Faulty field contactor.	Tighten or solder open or loose connections. Repair or replace defective rotor coils. Be sure field contactor is operating properly.
Overloaded	Check meter readings against nameplate ratings. Reduce load or install larger motor.

31. No Field Excitation

Probable cause	Remedy
Grounded or open rotor coil	Repair or replace rotor coil or coils.
Grounded or short sliprings	Check and reinsulate.
No output from exciter	See dc generator (par. 1).

141

32. Pulls out of Step, or Trips Breakers

Probable cause	*Remedy*
Low exciter voltage	Readjust voltage regulator on exciter to increase voltage.
Intermittently open or shorted cables	Check, and replace defective cables.
Reversed field coil	Check polarity. Change coil leads.
Low supply voltage	Increase voltage if possible. Raise excitation voltage.

33. Hunting

Probable cause	*Remedy*
Fluctuating load	Increase or decrease size of flywheel on load or loads. Increase or decrease excitation current.
Uneven commutator	Recondition commutator.

34. Stator Overheats in Spots

Probable cause	*Remedy*
Open phase coil	Check and repair or replace faulty coil or coils.
Rotor not centered	Check for bent shaft, loose or worn bearings. Straighten and realine shaft. Replace bearings.
Unbalanced circuits	Repair loose connections, or correct wrong internal connections.
Shorted coil	Check and replace faulty coil or coils.

35. Field Overheats

Probable cause	*Remedy*
Shorted field coil	Check and replace faulty coil or coils.
Excitation current too high	Reduce exciter current by adjusting dc voltage regulator.

36. Overheating

Probable cause	*Remedy*
Overloaded	Check meter readings against nameplate ratings. Reduce load or install larger motor.
Underexcited rotor	Adjust to rated excitation.
Improper ventilation	Remove obstructions and clean air ducts.
Improper supply voltage	Adjust to rated voltage.
Reverse field coil	Check polarity. Change coil leads.

Section VII.   AC REPULSION-INDUCTION MOTORS

37. Failure to Start

Probable cause	*Remedy*
Open fuse	Replace fuse.
Overloaded	Check meter readings against nameplate ratings. Reduce load or install larger motor.
Low supply voltage. Lead wires insufficient current capacity.	Apply correct voltage. Install larger lead wires.
Stator coil open	Check and replace open coil or coils.
Stator coil shorted	Check and replace shorted coil or coils.
Stator coil grounded	Check and replace defective coil or coils.
Centrifugal mechanism not operating properly	Disassemble, clean, inspect, adjust, repair or replace.
Incorrect brush setting	Locate neutral plane by shifting brushes until there is no rotation when current is applied. Shift brushes in the direction of the desired rotation, 1⅓ bars from neutral on 4-pole motors of ½ hp and smaller, and 1¾ bars on larger 4-pole motors. On 2-pole motors, set ⅓ bar farther than setting given above.
Bearings	Check for bent shaft or worn, loose, dry, or overlubricated bearing. Straighten and realine bent shaft. Replace worn and loose bearings, lubricate dry bearings, relieve overlubrication.

38. Runs Slow

Probable cause	Remedy
Overloaded	Check meter readings against nameplate rating.
Centrifugal mechanism not operating properly	Disassemble and clean.
Bearings binding	Clean and lubricate bearings.

39. Overheating

Probable cause	Remedy
Overloaded	Check meter readings against nameplate ratings. Reduce load or install larger motor.
Incorrect supply voltage	Apply correct voltage.
Centrifugal mechanism not operating properly	Disassemble, clean, inspect. Repair, adjust, or replace.
Bearings	Check for bent shaft, or worn, loose, dry, or overlubricated bearings. Straighten and realine bent shaft. Replace worn or loose bearings, lubricate dry bearings, relieve overlubrication.

40. Noisy Operation

Probable cause	Remedy
Bearings	Check for bent shaft, or worn, loose, dry, or overlubricated bearings. Straighten and realine bent shaft. Replace worn or loose bearings, lubricate dry bearings, relieve overlubrication.
Excessive end play	Adjust end-play takeup screw, or add thrust washers to shaft.
Motor not alined properly with driven machine	Realine.
Loose motor mounting and accessories	Tighten all loose components.

41. Motor Produces Shock when Touched

Probable cause	Remedy
Grounded stator coil	Replace defective coil or coils. Check motor-frame connection or connections to ground. Clean and tighten.
Static charge	Check motor-frame connection or connections to ground. Clean and tighten.

Section VIII.   AC SPLIT-PHASE, CAPACITOR-START, AND TRANSFORMER-CAPACITOR MOTORS

42. Failure to Start

Probable cause	Remedy
Open fuse	Replace fuse.
Low supply voltage	Apply correct voltage.
Stator coil open	Replace open coil or coils.
Centrifugal mechanism not operating properly	Disassemble, clean, inspect. Adjust, repair, or replace.
Defective capacitor	Replace capacitor.
Stator coil grounded	Check and replace grounded coil or coils.
Bearings	Check for bent shaft, or worn, loose, dry, or overlubricated bearings. Straighten and realine bent shaft. Replace worn or loose bearings, relieve overlubrication.
Overloaded	Check meter readings against nameplate ratings. Reduce load or install larger motor.

43. Overheating

Probable cause	Remedy
Shorted coil	Replace shorted coil or coils.
Centrifugal mechanism not operating properly	Disassemble, clean, inspect. Adjust, repair, or replace.
Incorrect voltage	Apply correct voltage.
Overloaded	Check meter readings against nameplate ratings. Reduce load or install larger motor.
Bearings	Check for bent shaft, or worn, loose, dry, or overlubricated bearings. Straighten and realine bent shaft, replace worn or loose bearings, lubricate dry bearings, relieve overlubrication.

44. Noisy Operation

Probable cause	Remedy
Worn bearings	Replace. Realine.
Shaft bent	Straighten shaft. Realine or replace rotor.
Excessive end play	Adjust screw of end-play takeup device, or put shim washers on shaft between end bells and rotor.
Loose motor mounts or accessories	Tighten all loose components.

II. TROUBLESHOOTING DATA FOR DC AND AC CONTROLLERS

Section I. DC CONTROLLERS

45. Failure to Close

Probable cause	*Remedy*
No power	Check power source. Replace faulty fuses.
Low voltage	Check power-supply voltage. Apply correct voltage.
Inadequate lead wires	Install lead wires of proper size.
Loose connections	Tighten all connections.
Open connections and broken wiring	Locate and repair or replace. Remove dirt from controller contacts.
Contacts affected by long idleness or high operating temperature.	Clean and adjust.
Contacts affected by chemical fumes or salty atmosphere.	Replace with oil-immersed contacts.
Inadequate contact pressure	Replace contacts and adjust spring tension.
Open circuit breaker	Check circuit wiring for possible fault.
Defective coil	Replace with new coil.
Overload-relay contact latched open	Operate hand- or electric-reset.

46. Failure to Open

Probable cause	*Remedy*
Interlock does not open circuit	Check control-circuit wiring for possible fault. Test and repair.
Holding circuit grounded	Test and repair or replace grounded parts.
Misalinement of parts; contacts apparently held together by residual magnetism.	Realine and test for free movement by hand. Magnetic sticking rarely occurs unless caused by excessive mechanical friction or misalinement of moving parts.
Contacts welded together	See paragraph 50, below.

47. Sluggish Operation

Probable cause	*Remedy*
Spring tension too strong	Adjust for proper spring tension.
Low voltage	Check power-supply voltage. Apply correct voltage.
Operating in wrong position	Remount in correct operating position.
Excessive friction	Realine and test for free movement by hand. Clean pivots.
Rusty parts due to long periods of idleness	Clean and renew rusty parts.
Sticky moving parts	Wipe off all accumulations of oil and dirt. Bearings do not need lubrication.
Misalinement of parts	Check for proper alinement. Realine to reduce friction, and test for free movement by hand.

48. Erratic Operation (Unwanted openings and closures, and failure of overload protection)

Probable cause	*Remedy*
Short circuits	Test and repair or replace defective parts.
Grounds	Test and repair or replace defective parts.

Probable cause	Remedy
Sneak currents	These are usually caused by intermittent grounds or short circuits in the machines or wiring circuit. Test and replace faulty parts or wiring.
Loose connections	Tighten all connections. Eliminate any vibrations or rapid temperature changes that may occur in close proximity to the controller.

49. Overheating of Coils

Probable cause	Remedy
Shorted coil	Replace coil.
High ambient temperature or poor ventilation	Relocate controller, use forced ventilation, or replace with suitable type controller.
High voltage	Check for shorted control resistor. Check power-supply voltage. Apply correct voltage.
High current	Check current rating of controller. Check for high voltage, above. If necessary, replace with suitable type controller.
Loose connections	Tighten all connections. Check for undue vibrations in vicinity.
Excessive collection of dirt and grime	Clean but do not reoil parts. If covers do not fit tightly, realine and adjust fasteners.
High humidity, extremely dirty atmosphere, excessive condensation, and rapid temperature changes.	Use oil-immersed controller or dusttight enclosures.

50. Contacts Welded Together

Probable cause	Remedy
Improper application	Check load conditions and replace with a suitable type controller.
Excessive temperature	Smooth off contact surface to remove concentrated hot spots.
Excessive binding of contact tip upon closing	Adjust spring pressure.
Contacts close without enough spring pressure	Replace worn contacts. Adjust or replace weak springs. Check armature overtravel.
Sluggish operation	See paragraph 47, above.
Rapid, momentary, touching of contacts without enough pressure.	Smooth contacts. Adjust weak springs. Where controller has "JOG" or "INCH" control button, operate this less rapidly.

51. Overheating of Contacts

Probable cause	Remedy
Inadequate spring pressure	Replace worn contacts. Adjust or replace weak springs.
Contacts overloaded	Check load data with controller rating. Replace with correct size contactor.
Dirty contacts	Clean and smooth contacts.
High humidity, extremely dirty atmosphere, excessive condensation, and rapid temperature changes.	See paragraph 49, above.
High ambient temperature or poor ventilation	See paragraph 49, above.
Chronic arcing	Adjust or replace arc chutes. If arcing persists, replace with a more suitable controller.
Rough contact surface	Clean and smooth contacts. Check alinement.
Continuous vibration when contacts are closed	Change or improve mounting of controller.
Oxidation of contacts	Keep clean, reduce excessive temperature, or use oil-immersed contacts.

52. Excessive Arcing of Contacts

Probable cause	Remedy
Arc not confined to proper path	Adjust or renew arc chutes. If arcing persists, replace with more suitable controller.
Inadequate spring pressure	Replace worn contacts. Adjust or replace weak springs.
Slow in opening	Remove excessive friction. Adjust spring tension. Renew weak springs. See paragraph 47, above.
Faulty blowout coil or connection	Check and replace coil. Tighten connection.
Excessive inductance in load circuit	Adjust load or replace with proper size controller.
Faulty capacitor	Replace with new capacitor.

53. Pitting or Corroding of Contacts

Probable cause	Remedy
Too little surface contact	Clean contacts and adjust springs.
Service too severe	Check load conditions and replace with correct size controller.
Corrosive atmosphere	Use airtight enclosure. In extreme cases, use oil-immersed contacts.
Continuous vibration when contacts are closed	Change, or improve, mounting of controller.
Oxidation of contacts	Keep clean, reduce excessive temperature, or use oil-immersed contacts.

Section II. AC CONTROLLERS

54. Failure to Close

Probable cause	Remedy
No power	Check power source. Replace faulty fuses.
Low voltage	Check power-supply voltage. Apply correct voltage. Check for low power factor.
Inadequate lead wires	Install lead wires of proper size.
Loose connections	Tighten all connections.
Open connections and broken wiring	Locate opens and repair or replace wiring. Remove dirt from controller contacts.
Contacts affected by long idleness or high operating temperature.	Clean and adjust.
Contacts affected by chemical fumes or salty atmosphere.	Replace with oil-immersed contacts.
Inadequate contact pressure	Replace contacts and adjust spring tension.
Open circuit breaker	Check circuit wiring for possible fault.
Defective coil	Replace with new coil.
Overload-relay contact latched open	Operate hand- or electric-reset.

55. Failure to Open

Probable cause	Remedy
Interlock does not open circuit	Check control-circuit wiring for possible fault. Test and repair.
Holding circuit grounded	Test and repair or replace grounded parts.
Misalinement of parts; contacts apparently held together by residual magnetism.	Realine and test for free movement by hand. Magnetic sticking rarely occurs unless caused by excessive mechanical friction or misalinement of moving parts. Wipe off pole faces to remove accumulation of oil.
Contacts welded together	See paragraph 59, below.

56. Sluggish Operation

Probable cause	Remedy
Spring tension too strong	Adjust for proper spring tension.
Low voltage	Check power-supply voltage. Apply correct voltage.
Operating in wrong position	Remount in correct operating position.
Excessive friction	Realine and test for free movement by hand. Clean pivots.
Rusty parts due to long periods of idleness	Clean or renew rusty parts.
Sticky moving parts	Wipe off all accumulations of oil and dirt. Bearings do not need lubrication.
Misalinement of parts	Check for proper alinement. Realine to reduce friction and test for free movement by hand.

57. Erratic Operation (Unwanted openings and closures and failure of overload protection)

Probable cause	Remedy
Short circuits	Test and repair or replace defective parts.
Grounds	Test and repair or replace defective parts.
Sneak currents	These are usually caused by intermittent grounds or short circuits in the machines or wiring circuit. Test and replace faulty parts or wiring.
Loose connections	Tighten all connections. Eliminate any vibrations or rapid temperature changes that may occur in close proximity to the controller.

58. Overheating of Coils

Probable cause	Remedy
Shorted coil	Replace coil.
High ambient temperature or poor ventilation	Relocate controller, use forced ventilation, or replace with suitable type controller.
High voltage	Check for shorted control resistor. Check power-supply voltage. Apply correct voltage.
High current	Check current rating of controller. Make check for high voltage, above. If necessary, replace with suitable type controller.
Loose connections	Tighten all connections. Check for undue vibrations in vicinity.
Excessive collection of dirt and grime	Clean but do not reoil parts. If covers do not fit tightly, realine and adjust fasteners.
High humidity, extremely dirty atmosphere, excessive condensation, and rapid temperature changes.	Use oil-immersed controller or dusttight enclosures.
Operating on wrong frequency	Replace with coil of proper frequency rating.
DC instead of ac coil	Replace with ac coil.
Too frequent operation	Adjust to apply larger control.
Open armature gap	Adjust spring tension. Eliminate excessive friction or remove any blocking in gap.

59. Contacts Welded Together

Probable cause	Remedy
Improper application	Check load conditions and replace with a more suitable type controller.
Excessive temperature	Smooth off contact surface to remove concentrated hot spots.
Excessive binding of contact tip upon closing	Adjust spring pressure.
Contacts close without enough spring pressure	Replace worn contacts. Adjust or replace weak springs. Check armature overtravel.
Sluggish operation	See paragraph 56, above.
Rapid, momentary, touching of contacts without enough pressure.	Smooth contacts. Adjust weak springs. Where controller has "JOG" or "INCH" control button, operate this less rapidly.

60. Overheating or Contacts

Probable cause	Remedy
Inadequate spring pressure	Replace worn contacts. Adjust or replace weak springs.
Contacts overloaded	Check load data with controller rating. Replace with correct size contactor.
Dirty contacts	Clean and smooth contacts.
High humidity, extremely dirty atmosphere, excessive condensation, and rapid temperature changes.	See paragraph 58, above.
High ambient temperature or poor ventilation	See paragraph 58, above.
Chronic arcing	Adjust or replace arc chutes. If arcing persists, replace with a more suitable controller.

Probable cause	*Remedy*
Rough contact surfaces	Clean and smooth contacts. Check alinement.
Continuous vibration when contacts are closed	Change or improve mounting of controller.
Oxidation of contacts	Keep clean, reduce excessive temperature, or use oil-immersed contacts.

61. Arcing at Contacts

Probable cause	*Remedy*
Arc not confined to proper path	Adjust or renew arc chutes. If arcing persists, replace with more suitable controller.
Inadequate spring pressure	Replace worn contacts. Adjust or replace weak springs.
Slow in opening	Remove excessive friction. Adjust spring tension. Renew weak springs. See paragraph 56, above.
Faulty blowout coil or connection	Check and replace coil. Tighten connection.
Excessive inductance in load circuit	Adjust load or replace with more suitable controller.

62. Pitting or Corroding of Contacts

Probable cause	*Remedy*
Too little surface contact	Clean contacts and adjust springs.
Service too severe	Check load conditions and replace with more suitable controller.
Corrosive atmosphere	Use airtight enclosure. In extreme cases, use oil-immersed contacts.
Continuous vibration when contacts are closed	Change or improve mounting of controller.
Oxidation of contacts	Keep clean, reduce excessive temperature, or use oil-immersed contacts.

63. Noisy Operation (Hum or Chatter)

Probable cause	*Remedy*
Poor fit at pole face	Realine and adjust pole faces.
Broken or defective shading coil	Replace coil.
Loose coil	Check coil. If correct size, shim coil until tight.
Worn parts	Replace with new parts.

64. Vibration After Repairs

Probable cause	*Remedy*
Misalinement of parts	Realine parts and test for free movement by hand.
Loose mounting	Tighten mounting bolts.
Incorrect coil	Replace with proper coil.
Too much play in moving parts	Shim parts for proper tightness and clearance.

ANSWER SHEET

TEST NO. _____ PART _____ TITLE OF POSITION _____

PLACE OF EXAMINATION _____ DATE _____

(CITY OR TOWN)   (STATE)

RATING

USE THE SPECIAL PENCIL.   MAKE GLOSSY BLACK MARKS.

	A B C D E		A B C D E		A B C D E		A B C D E		A B C D E
1		26		51		76		101	
2		27		52		77		102	
3		28		53		78		103	
4		29		54		79		104	
5		30		55		80		105	
6		31		56		81		106	
7		32		57		82		107	
8		33		58		83		108	
9		34		59		84		109	
10		35		60		85		110	

Make only ONE mark for each answer.   Additional and stray marks may be
counted as mistakes.   In making corrections, erase errors COMPLETELY.

	A B C D E		A B C D E		A B C D E		A B C D E		A B C D E
11		36		61		86		111	
12		37		62		87		112	
13		38		63		88		113	
14		39		64		89		114	
15		40		65		90		115	
16		41		66		91		116	
17		42		67		92		117	
18		43		68		93		118	
19		44		69		94		119	
20		45		70		95		120	
21		46		71		96		121	
22		47		72		97		122	
23		48		73		98		123	
24		49		74		99		124	
25		50		75		100		125	

150

ELECTRICAL TERMS AND FORMULAS

CONTENTS

	Page
TERMS	1
Agonic ...... Dielectric	1
Diode ...... Lead	2
Line of Force ...... Resistor	3
Retentivity ...... Wattmeter	4
FORMULAS	4
Ohm's Law for D-C Circuits	4
Resistors in Series	4
Resistors in Parallel	4
R-L Circuit Time Constant	5
R-C Circuit Time Constant	5
Comparison of Units in Electric and Magnetic Circuits	5
Capacitors in Series	5
Capacitors in Parallel	5
Capacitive Reactance	5
Impedance in an R-C Circuit (Series)	5
Inductors in Series	5
Inductors in Parallel	5
Inductive Reactance	5
Q of a Coil	5
Impedance of an R-L Circuit (Series)	5
Impedance with R, C, and L in Series	5
Parallel Circuit Impedance	5
Sine-Wave Voltage Relationships	5
Power in A-C Circuit	6
Transformers	6
Three-Phase Voltage and Current Relationships	6
GREEK ALPHABET	7
Alpha ...... Omega	7
COMMON ABBREVIATIONS AND LETTER SYMBOLS	8
Alternating Current (noun) ...... Watt	8

ELECTRICAL TERMS AND FORMULAS

Terms

AGONIC.—An imaginary line of the earth's surface passing through points where the magnetic declination is 0°; that is, points where the compass points to true north.

AMMETER.—An instrument for measuring the amount of electron flow in amperes.

AMPERE.—The basic unit of electrical current.

AMPERE-TURN.—The magnetizing force produced by a current of one ampere flowing through a coil of one turn.

AMPLIDYNE.—A rotary magnetic or dynamo-electric amplifier used in servomechanism and control applications.

AMPLIFICATION.—The process of increasing the strength (current, power, or voltage) of a signal.

AMPLIFIER.—A device used to increase the signal voltage, current, or power, generally composed of a vacuum tube and associated circuit called a stage. It may contain several stages in order to obtain a desired gain.

AMPLITUDE.—The maximum instantaneous value of an alternating voltage or current, measured in either the positive or negative direction.

ARC.—A flash caused by an electric current ionizing a gas or vapor.

ARMATURE.—The rotating part of an electric motor or generator. The moving part of a relay or vibrator.

ATTENUATOR.—A network of resistors used to reduce voltage, current, or power delivered to a load.

AUTOTRANSFORMER.—A transformer in which the primary and secondary are connected together in one winding.

BATTERY.—Two or more primary or secondary cells connected together electrically. The term does not apply to a single cell.

BREAKER POINTS.—Metal contacts that open and close a circuit at timed intervals.

BRIDGE CIRCUIT.—The electrical bridge circuit is a term referring to any one of a variety of electric circuit networks, one branch of which, the "bridge" proper, connects two points of equal potential and hence carries no current when the circuit is properly adjusted or balanced.

BRUSH.—The conducting material, usually a block of carbon, bearing against the commutator or sliprings through which the current flows in or out.

BUS BAR.—A primary power distribution point connected to the main power source.

CAPACITOR.—Two electrodes or sets of electrodes in the form of plates, separated from each other by an insulating material called the dielectric.

CHOKE COIL.—A coil of low ohmic resistance and high impedance to alternating current.

CIRCUIT.—The complete path of an electric current.

CIRCUIT BREAKER.—An electromagnetic or thermal device that opens a circuit when the current in the circuit exceeds a predetermined amount. Circuit breakers can be reset.

CIRCULAR MIL.—An area equal to that of a circle with a diameter of 0.001 inch. It is used for measuring the cross section of wires.

COAXIAL CABLE.—A transmission line consisting of two conductors concentric with and insulated from each other.

COMMUTATOR.—The copper segments on the armature of a motor or generator. It is cylindrical in shape and is used to pass power into or from the brushes. It is a switching device.

CONDUCTANCE.—The ability of a material to conduct or carry an electric current. It is the reciprocal of the resistance of the material, and is expressed in mhos.

CONDUCTIVITY.—The ease with which a substance transmits electricity.

CONDUCTOR.—Any material suitable for carrying electric current.

CORE.—A magnetic material that affords an easy path for magnetic flux lines in a coil.

COUNTER E.M.F.—Counter electromotive force; an e.m.f. induced in a coil or armature that opposes the applied voltage.

CURRENT LIMITER.—A protective device similar to a fuse, usually used in high amperage circuits.

CYCLE.—One complete positive and one complete negative alternation of a current or voltage.

DIELECTRIC.—An insulator; a term that refers to the insulating material between the plates of a capacitor.

ELECTRICAL TERMS AND FORMULAS

DIODE.—Vacuum tube—a two element tube that contains a cathode and plate; semiconductor —a material of either germanium or silicon that is manufactured to allow current to flow in only one direction. Diodes are used as rectifiers and detectors.

DIRECT CURRENT.—An electric current that flows in one direction only.

EDDY CURRENT.—Induced circulating currents in a conducting material that are caused by a varying magnetic field.

EFFICIENCY.—The ratio of output power to input power, generally expressed as a percentage.

ELECTROLYTE.—A solution of a substance which is capable of conducting electricity. An electrolyte may be in the form of either a liquid or a paste.

ELECTROMAGNET.—A magnet made by passing current through a coil of wire wound on a soft iron core.

ELECTROMOTIVE FORCE (e.m.f.).—The force that produces an electric current in a circuit.

ELECTRON.—A negatively charged particle of matter.

ENERGY.—The ability or capacity to do work.

FARAD.—The unit of capacitance.

FEEDBACK.—A transfer of energy from the output circuit of a device back to its input.

FIELD.—The space containing electric or magnetic lines of force.

FIELD WINDING.—The coil used to provide the magnetizing force in motors and generators.

FLUX FIELD.—All electric or magnetic lines of force in a given region.

FREE ELECTRONS.—Electrons which are loosely held and consequently tend to move at random among the atoms of the material.

FREQUENCY.—The number of complete cycles per second existing in any form of wave motion; such as the number of cycles per second of an alternating current.

FULL-WAVE RECTIFIER CIRCUIT.—A circuit which utilizes both the positive and the negative alternations of an alternating current to produce a direct current.

FUSE.—A protective device inserted in series with a circuit. It contains a metal that will melt or break when current is increased beyond a specific value for a definite period of time.

GAIN.—The ratio of the output power, voltage, or current to the input power, voltage, or current, respectively.

GALVANOMETER.—An instrument used to measure small d-c currents.

GENERATOR.—A machine that converts mechanical energy into electrical energy.

GROUND.—A metallic connection with the earth to establish ground potential. Also, a common return to a point of zero potential. The chassis of a receiver or a transmitter is sometimes the common return, and therefore the ground of the unit.

HENRY.—The basic unit of inductance.

HORSEPOWER.—The English unit of power, equal to work done at the rate of 550 foot-pounds per second. Equal to 746 watts of electrical power.

HYSTERESIS.—A lagging of the magnetic flux in a magnetic material behind the magnetizing force which is producing it.

IMPEDANCE.—The total opposition offered to the flow of an alternating current. It may consist of any combination of resistance, inductive reactance, and capacitive reactance.

INDUCTANCE.—The property of a circuit which tends to oppose a change in the existing current.

INDUCTION.—The act or process of producing voltage by the relative motion of a magnetic field across a conductor.

INDUCTIVE REACTANCE.—The opposition to the flow of alternating or pulsating current caused by the inductance of a circuit. It is measured in ohms.

INPHASE.—Applied to the condition that exists when two waves of the same frequency pass through their maximum and minimum values of like polarity at the same instant.

INVERSELY.—Inverted or reversed in position or relationship.

ISOGONIC LINE.—An imaginary line drawn through points on the earth's surface where the magnetic deviation is equal.

JOULE.—A unit of energy or work. A joule of energy is liberated by one ampere flowing for one second through a resistance of one ohm.

KILO.—A prefix meaning 1,000.

LAG.—The amount one wave is behind another in time; expressed in electrical degrees.

LAMINATED CORE.—A core built up from thin sheets of metal and used in transformers and relays.

LEAD.—The opposite of LAG. Also, a wire or connection.

ELECTRICAL TERMS AND FORMULAS

LINE OF FORCE.-A line in an electric or magnetic field that shows the direction of the force.

LOAD.-The power that is being delivered by any power producing device. The equipment that uses the power from the power producing device.

MAGNETIC AMPLIFIER.-A saturable reactor type device that is used in a circuit to amplify or control.

MAGNETIC CIRCUIT.-The complete path of magnetic lines of force.

MAGNETIC FIELD.-The space in which a magnetic force exists.

MAGNETIC FLUX.-The total number of lines of force issuing from a pole of a magnet.

MAGNETIZE.-To convert a material into a magnet by causing the molecules to rearrange.

MAGNETO.-A generator which produces alternating current and has a permanent magnet as its field.

MEGGER.-A test instrument used to measure insulation resistance and other high resistances. It is a portable hand operated d-c generator used as an ohmmeter.

MEGOHM.-A million ohms.

MICRO.-A prefix meaning one-millionth.

MILLI.-A prefix meaning one-thousandth.

MILLIAMMETER.-An ammeter that measures current in thousandths of an ampere.

MOTOR-GENERATOR.-A motor and a generator with a common shaft used to convert line voltages to other voltages or frequencies.

MUTUAL INDUCTANCE.-A circuit property existing when the relative position of two inductors causes the magnetic lines of force from one to link with the turns of the other.

NEGATIVE CHARGE.-The electrical charge carried by a body which has an excess of electrons.

NEUTRON.-A particle having the weight of a proton but carrying no electric charge. It is located in the nucleus of an atom.

NUCLEUS.-The central part of an atom that is mainly comprised of protons and neutrons. It is the part of the atom that has the most mass.

NULL.-Zero.

OHM.-The unit of electrical resistance.

OHMMETER.-An instrument for directly measuring resistance in ohms.

OVERLOAD.-A load greater than the rated load of an electrical device.

PERMALLOY.-An alloy of nickel and iron having an abnormally high magnetic permeability.

PERMEABILITY.-A measure of the ease with which magnetic lines of force can flow through a material as compared to air.

PHASE DIFFERENCE.-The time in electrical degrees by which one wave leads or lags another.

POLARITY.-The character of having magnetic poles, or electric charges.

POLE.-The section of a magnet where the flux lines are concentrated; also where they enter and leave the magnet. An electrode of a battery.

POLYPHASE.-A circuit that utilizes more than one phase of alternating current.

POSITIVE CHARGE.-The electrical charge carried by a body which has become deficient in electrons.

POTENTIAL.-The amount of charge held by a body as compared to another point or body. Usually measured in volts.

POTENTIOMETER.-A variable voltage divider; a resistor which has a variable contact arm so that any portion of the potential applied between its ends may be selected.

POWER.-The rate of doing work or the rate of expending energy. The unit of electrical power is the watt.

POWER FACTOR.-The ratio of the actual power of an alternating or pulsating current, as measured by a wattmeter, to the apparent power, as indicated by ammeter and voltmeter readings. The power factor of an inductor, capacitor, or insulator is an expression of their losses.

PRIME MOVER.-The source of mechanical power used to drive the rotor of a generator.

PROTON.-A positively charged particle in the nucleus of an atom.

RATIO.-The value obtained by dividing one number by another, indicating their relative proportions.

REACTANCE.-The opposition offered to the flow of an alternating current by the inductance, capacitance, or both, in any circuit.

RECTIFIERS.-Devices used to change alternating current to unidirectional current. These may be vacuum tubes, semiconductors such as germanium and silicon, and dry-disk rectifiers such as selenium and copper-oxide.

RELAY.-An electromechanical switching device that can be used as a remote control.

RELUCTANCE.-A measure of the opposition that a material offers to magnetic lines of force.

RESISTANCE.-The opposition to the flow of current caused by the nature and physical dimensions of a conductor.

RESISTOR.-A circuit element whose chief characteristic is resistance; used to oppose the flow of current.

4
4

ELECTRICAL TERMS AND FORMULAS

RETENTIVITY.—The measure of the ability of a material to hold its magnetism.

RHEOSTAT.—A variable resistor.

SATURABLE REACTOR.—A control device that uses a small d-c current to control a large a-c current by controlling core flux density.

SATURATION.—The condition existing in any circuit when an increase in the driving signal produces no further change in the resultant effect.

SELF-INDUCTION.—The process by which a circuit induces an e.m.f. into itself by its own magnetic field.

SERIES-WOUND.—A motor or generator in which the armature is wired in series with the field winding.

SERVO.—A device used to convert a small movement into one of greater movement or force.

SERVOMECHANISM.—A closed-loop system that produces a force to position an object in accordance with the information that originates at the input.

SOLENOID.—An electromagnetic coil that contains a movable plunger.

SPACE CHARGE.—The cloud of electrons existing in the space between the cathode and plate in a vacuum tube, formed by the electrons emitted from the cathode in excess of those immediately attracted to the plate.

SPECIFIC GRAVITY—The ratio between the density of a substance and that of pure water, at a given temperature.

SYNCHROSCOPE—An instrument used to indicate a difference in frequency between two a-c sources.

SYNCHRO SYSTEM.—An electrical system that gives remote indications or control by means of self-synchronizing motors.

TACHOMETER.—An instrument for indicating revolutions per minute.

TERTIARY WINDING.—A third winding on a transformer or magnetic amplifier that is used as a second control winding.

THERMISTOR.—A resistor that is used to compensate for temperature variations in a circuit.

THERMOCOUPLE.—A junction of two dissimilar metals that produces a voltage when heated.

TORQUE.—The turning effort or twist which a shaft sustains when transmitting power.

TRANSFORMER.—A device composed of two or more coils, linked by magnetic lines of force, used to transfer energy from one circuit to another.

TRANSMISSION LINES.—Any conductor or system of conductors used to carry electrical energy from its source to a load.

VARS.—Abbreviation for volt-ampere, reactive.

VECTOR.—A line used to represent both direction and magnitude.

VOLT.—The unit of electrical potential.

VOLTMETER.—An instrument designed to measure a difference in electrical potential, in volts.

WATT.—The unit of electrical power.

WATTMETER.—An instrument for measuring electrical power in watts.

Formulas

Ohm's Law for d-c Circuits

$$I = \frac{E}{R} = \frac{P}{E} = \sqrt{\frac{P}{R}}$$

$$R = \frac{E}{I} = \frac{P}{I^2} = \frac{E^2}{P}$$

$$E = IR = \frac{P}{I} = \sqrt{PR}$$

$$P = EI = \frac{E^2}{R} = I^2R$$

Resistors in Series

$$R_T = R_1 + R_2 \cdots$$

Resistors in Parallel
Two resistors

$$R_T = \frac{R_1 R_2}{R_1 + R_2}$$

More than two

$$\frac{1}{R_T} = \frac{1}{R_1} + \frac{1}{R_2} + \frac{1}{R_3}$$

156

ELECTRICAL TERMS AND FORMULAS

R-L Circuit Time Constant equals

$\dfrac{L \text{ (in henrys)}}{R \text{ (in ohms)}} = t$ (in seconds), or

$\dfrac{L \text{ (in microhenrys)}}{R \text{ (in ohms)}} = t$ (in microseconds)

R-C Circuit Time Constant equals

R (ohms) X C (farads) $=$ t (seconds)

R (megohms) x C (microfarads) $=$ t (seconds)

R (ohms) x C (microfarads) $=$ t (microseconds)

R (megohms) x C (micromicrofrads $=$ t (microseconds)

Comparison of Units in Electric and Magnetic Circuits.

	Electric circuit	Magnetic circuit
Force	Volt, E or e.m.f.	Gilberts, F, or m.m.f.
Flow	Ampere, I	Flux, Φ, in maxwells
Opposition	Ohms, R	Reluctance, R
Law	Ohm's law, $I = \dfrac{E}{R}$	Rowland's law $\Phi = \dfrac{F}{R}$
Intensity of force	Volts per cm. of length	$H = \dfrac{1.257IN}{L}$, gilberts per centimeter of length
Density	Current density— for example, amperes per cm^2.	Flux density—for example, lines per cm^2., or gausses

Capacitors in Series
  Two capacitors

$$C_T = \frac{C_1 C_2}{C_1 + C_2}$$

  More than two

$$\frac{1}{C_T} = \frac{1}{C_1} + \frac{1}{C_2} + \frac{1}{C_3}\cdots$$

Capacitors in Parallel

$$C_T = C_1 + C_2\cdots$$

Capacitive Reactance

$$X_c = \frac{1}{2\pi fC}$$

Impedance in an R-C Circuit (Series)

$$Z = \sqrt{R^2 + X_c^2}$$

Inductors in Series

$$L_T = L_1 + L_2 \ldots \text{(No coupling between coils)}$$

Inductors in Parallel
  Two inductors

$$L_T = \frac{L_1 L_2}{L_1 + L_2} \text{(No coupling between coils)}$$

More than two

$$\frac{1}{L_T} = \frac{1}{L_1} + \frac{1}{L_2} + \frac{1}{L_3} \ldots \text{(No coupling between coils)}$$

Inductive Reactance

$$X_L = 2\pi fL$$

Q of a Coil

$$Q = \frac{X_L}{R}$$

Impedance of an R-L Circuit (series)

$$Z = \sqrt{R^2 + X_L^2}$$

Impedance with R, C, and L in Series

$$Z = \sqrt{R^2 + (X_L - X_C)^2}$$

Parallel Circuit Impedance

$$Z = \frac{Z_1 Z_2}{Z_1 + Z_2}$$

Sine-Wave Voltage Relationships
  Average value

$$E_{ave} = \frac{2}{\pi} \times E_{max} = 0.637 E_{max}$$

ELECTRICAL TERMS AND FORMULAS

Effective or r.m.s. value

$$E_{eff} = \frac{E_{max}}{\sqrt{2}} = \frac{E_{max}}{1.414} = 0.707 E_{max} = 1.11 E_{ave}$$

Maximum value

$$E_{max} = \sqrt{2} E_{eff} = 1.414 E_{eff} = 1.57 E_{ave}$$

Voltage in an a-c circuit

$$E = IZ = \frac{P}{I \times P.F.}$$

Current in an a-c circuit

$$I = \frac{E}{Z} = \frac{P}{E \times P.F.}$$

Power in A-C Circuit
Apparent power $= EI$
True power

$$P = EI \cos \theta = EI \times P.F.$$

Power factor

$$P.F. = \frac{P}{EI} = \cos \theta$$

$$\cos \theta = \frac{true\ power}{apparent\ power}$$

Transformers
Voltage relationship

$$\frac{E}{E} = \frac{N}{N} \text{ or } E = E \times \frac{N}{N}$$

Current relationship

$$\frac{I_p}{I_s} = \frac{N_s}{N_p}$$

Induced voltage

$$E_{eff} = 4.44\, BAfN\, 10^{-8}$$

Turns ratio equals

$$\frac{N_p}{N_s} = \sqrt{\frac{Z_p}{Z_s}}$$

Secondary current

$$I_s = I_p \frac{N_p}{N_s}$$

Secondary voltage

$$E_s = E_p \frac{N_s}{N_p}$$

Three Phase Voltage and Current Relationships
With wye connected windings

$$E_{line} = 1.732 E_{coil} = \sqrt{3} E_{coil}$$

$$I_{line} = I_{coil}$$

With delta connected windings

$$E_{line} = E_{coil}$$

$$I_{line} = 1.732 I_{coil}$$

With wye or delta connected winding

$$P_{coil} = E_{coil} I_{coil}$$

$$P_t = 3 P_{coil}$$

$$P_t = 1.732 E_{line} I_{line}$$

(To convert to true power multiply by $\cos \theta$)

Synchronous Speed of Motor

$$r.p.m. = \frac{120 \times frequency}{number\ of\ poles}$$

GREEK ALPHABET

Name	Capital	Lower Case	Designates
Alpha	A	α	Angles.
Beta	B	β	Angles, flux density.
Gamma . . .	Γ	γ	Conductivity.
Delta	Δ	δ	Variation of a quantity, increment.
Epsilon . . .	E	ϵ	Base of natural logarithms (2.71828).
Zeta	Z	ζ	Impedance, coefficients, coordinates.
Eta	H	η	Hysteresis coefficient, efficiency, magnetizing force.
Theta.	Θ	θ	Phase angle.
Iota	I	ι	
Kappa	K	κ	Dielectric constant, coupling coefficient, susceptibility.
Lambda . . .	Λ	λ	Wavelength.
Mu	M	μ	Permeability, micro, amplification factor.
Nu	N	ν	Reluctivity.
Xi	Ξ	ξ	
Omicron . . .	O	o	
Pi	Π	π	3.1416
Rho	P	ρ	Resistivity.
Sigma	Σ	σ	
Tau	T	τ	Time constant, time-phase displacement.
Upsilon . . .	Υ	υ	
Phi	Φ	φ	Angles, magnetic flux.
Chi	X	χ	
Psi	Ψ	ψ	Dielectric flux, phase difference.
Omega	Ω	ω	Ohms (capital), angular velocity (2 π f).

COMMON ABBREVIATIONS AND LETTER SYMBOLS

Term	Abbreviation or Symbol
alternating current (noun)	a,c.
alternating-current (adj.)	a-c
ampere	a.
area	A
audiofrequency (noun)	AF
audiofrequency (adj.)	A-F
capacitance	C
capacitive reactance	X_C
centimeter	cm.
conductance	G
coulomb	Q
counterelectromotive force	c.e.m.f.
current (d-c or r.m.s. value)	I
current (instantaneous value)	i
cycles per second	c.p.s.
dielectric constant	K,k
difference in potential (d-c or r.m.s. value)	E
difference in potential (instantaneous value)	e
direct current (noun)	d.c.
direct-current (adj.)	d-c
electromotive force	e.m.f.
frequency	f
henry	h.
horsepower	hp.
impedance	Z
inductance	L
inductive reactance	X_L
kilovolt	kv.
kilovolt-ampere	kv.-a.
kilowatt	kw.
kilowatt-hour	kw.-hr.
magnetic field intensity	H
magnetomotive force	m.m.f.
megohm	M
microampere	μ a.
microfarad	μ f.
microhenry	μ h.
micromicrofarad	$\mu\mu$ f.
microvolt	μ v.
milliampere	ma.
millihenry	mh.
milliwatt	mw.
mutual inductance	M
power	P
resistance	R
revolutions per minute	r.p.m.
root mean square	r.m.s.
time	t
torque	T
volt	v.
watt	w.